UNITING

WISDOM AND COMPASSION

UNITING

# WISDOM

AND

# COMPASSION

Illuminating

*The Thirty-Seven Practices*

*of a Bodhisattva*

CHÖKYI
DRAGPA

Introduction by
CHÖKYI NYIMA
RINPOCHE

Translated by
Heidi I. Köppl

Wisdom Publications • Boston

Wisdom Publications
199 Elm Street
Somerville, MA 02144 USA
www.wisdompubs.org

*Library of Congress Cataloging-in-Publication Data*
Thub-bstan-chos-kyi-grags-pa.
  Uniting wisdom and compassion : illuminating the thirty-seven
practices of a Bodhisattva / Chökyi Dragpa ; introduction by Chökyi
Nyima Rinpoche ; translated by Heidi I. Köppl.
    p. cm.
  ISBN 0-86171-377-X (pbk. : alk. paper)
  1. Enlightenment (Buddhism)—Requisites. 2. Spiritual life—Buddhism.
3. Bodhisattvas. I. Köppl, Heidi I. II. Title.
BQ4399 .T49 2004
294.3'444—dc22

                            2003025227


09 08 07 06 05 04
6  5  4  3  2  1

Cover design by Rick Snizik
Interior design by Potter Publishing Studio. Set in Aldine 401 10/13.

Wisdom Publications' books are printed on acid-free paper and meet the
guidelines for permanence and durability of the Committee on Production
Guidelines for Book Longevity of the Council on Library Resources.

Printed in Canada.

# TABLE OF CONTENTS

## PUBLISHER'S ACKNOWLEDGMENT

The Publisher gratefully acknowledges the generous help of the Hershey Family Foundation in sponsoring the publication of this book.

# TRANSLATOR'S PREFACE

## HISTORICAL NOTES

THE CLASSIC TEXT that forms the basis for the commentary translated here was composed by Gyalse Togme (1295–1369).[1] Known in the West as *The Thirty-Seven Practices of a Bodhisattva (Rgyal ba'i sras kyi lag len sum chu so bdun ma)*, this text beautifully portrays the central Mahayana thoughts of loving-kindness and compassion together with their cultivation through practice. Although the root text was composed some centuries ago, it remains highly relevant for modern readers due to its down-to-earth instructions and straightforward approach. Without much elaboration but with great literary beauty, it summarizes the quintessence of the Mahayana path in a way that has made it a dear treasure to spiritual practitioners throughout the centuries.

Here, it is presented with an extraordinary commentary by Tubten Chökyi Dragpa (died c. 1908).[2] The unique features of his commentary are not only a close reliance on the sutras and the Indian treatises to highlight the purport of Gyalse Togme's root verses, but especially its abundance of striking and at times unique advice from ancient masters of the Kadam tradition. The Kadam masters were renowned for giving pithy teachings in a language that is simple, direct, and sometimes even blunt.

Gyalse Togme lived at a time when the sectarian boundaries that characterized the later development of Buddhism in Tibet had not yet been fully drawn, and so an open-minded environment encouraged scholars to travel to various acclaimed monastic centers and pursue their studies in Buddhist philosophy regardless of the center's philosophical orientation. The period from the fifteenth to the seventeenth century was especially marred by sectarian rivalries, and it was not until the nineteenth century that a movement for nonsectarian appreciation for the diversity of traditions would come to the forefront again. Prominent eclectics such as Jamyang Khyentse Wangpo (1820–92) and Jamgon Kongtrul Lodrö Taye (1813–99) founded the well-known nonsectarian Rimé movement,[3] and it is in this relatively free-spirited and open-minded environment that we find the composer of this commentary.

Tubten Chökyi Dragpa, also known as Minyag Kunzang Sönam, originally a Gelug adherent, studied under the legendary yogin scholar and central representative of the Rimé movement, Dza Patrul Rinpoche (1820–92). Attending Patrul with perfect devotion for over twenty years, Tubten Chökyi Dragpa became renowned as the foremost of Paltrul's disciples from the Gelug tradition.[4]

In the nineteenth and twentieth centuries, when sectarian boundaries had become so clearly manifest, the masters of the Rimé movement proposed a turn away from the engraved distinctions by emphasizing the study of classical and universally treasured texts that dated before the Tibetan parochial demarcations. It is in this spirit that Chökyi Dragpa here comments on Gyalse Togme's *Thirty-Seven Practices*. While his own commentary on each root verse is rather short, his abundant use of classical scriptural statements and the instructions of the early Kadam masters become the highlights of his exposition.

The Kadampas were a reformist lineage founded by the Tibetan followers of the great Indian master Atisha (982–1054).[5] They strove to present the fundamentals of Buddhism in a way that was easily accessible to both ordained practitioners in monastic settings as well as the community of laypeople living a busy life in the world.[6] The methods developed for this purpose were codified by Atisha's Tibetan disciples[7] and came to form the unique literary genre of *mind training (blo sbyong)*.[8]

*The Thirty-Seven Practices,* however, is typically considered part of the literary genre of *lamrim* (stages of the path), laying out distinctively the different stages through which a spiritual practitioner ought to journey. In texts belonging to the lamrim genre we find explanations about three types of individuals: those of lower capacity ,those of medium capacity, and those of great capacity. The practitioner begins by training according to the way of the inferior type and gradually develops into a "great individual" who aspires to achieve buddhahood for the sake of all sentient beings. Although lamrim texts usually conclude with explanations of the esoteric path, we can see that *The Thirty-Seven Practices* only lays out the path of a bodhisattva according to the general Mahayana. The origin of this genre in Tibet is said to be Atisha's renowned *Bodhipathapradipa.*

Although this text can in this way clearly be seen as lamrim, we find throughout the verses strong elements of the mind training tradition. Taking this into account, and also that most of the abundant sayings and advice of the Kadampas found in the commentary are extracted from mind training texts, I would like to consider briefly here the origin and lineage of mind training.

The lineage of mind training in Tibet was transmitted by Atisha to his disciple Dromtonpa (1005–64), who is considered the primary founder of the Kadam school. Dromtonpa's three most renowned disciples, who because of their close spiritual kinship were known as the three brothers, were Puchungwa (1031–1106), Potowa (1027–1105), and Chen-ngawa (1033–1103). These were the primary forces in propagating the Kadam teachings. Another Kadam master of the eleventh century was the "little meditator" of Kharag, or Kharagpa, who was a disciple of Potowa. He was famous for his perseverance and strict application of the teachings, and it is said that he received teachings on the Great Perfection *(rdzogs chen)* and subsequently attained the form of enlightenment known as the *rainbow body.*[9]

Gonpawa (eleventh century) was another of Atisha's disciples who propagated the lineage of the Kadam lamrim. Langri Tangpa (1054–1123), a student of Potowa whom we also often see quoted, is the author of *The Eight Stanzas on Mind Training,* the first text to carry the title "mind training."

Langri Tangpa's student Sharawa (1070–1141),[10] also a student of Potowa, became the teacher of Chekawa (1101–75). Chekawa was inspired to study mind training after reading Langri Tangpa's *Eight Stanzas* and consequently composed the famous *Seven Points of Mind Training,* which was to inspire commentaries by famous masters of all Tibetan Buddhist schools, including Gyalse Togme, author of *The Thirty-Seven Practices.* Among later prominent commentators on the *Seven Points of Mind Training* we find the great forefathers of the Gelug school, Tsongkhapa (1357–1419) and Gendun Drub (1391–1474), and the Rimé masters Jamgon Kongtrul Lodrö Taye and Jamyang Khyentse Wangpo. Thus, mind training was generally considered an essential and all-important practice within all the schools of Tibetan Buddhism.

A FEW WORDS ARE IN ORDER regarding Gyalse Togme, the author of *The Thirty-Seven Practices.* The literal meaning of *gyalse* is "son of the victorious ones," a synonym for bodhisattva, and so his name is indicative of superior loving-kindness and compassion. *Togme* is the Tibetan version of the Sanskrit *Asanga,* which is the name of a renowned Indian Mahayana master of the fourth century. It is said that Gyalse Togme received the name Togme at a relatively young age while studying Asanga's *Abhidharma Compendium.*[11] His teacher asked the class about the meaning of the term "suffering without disturbance,"[12] but no one in the class was able to answer except Gyalse Togme. He explained that this referred to the type of suffering that can still be experienced by an *arhat* as a result of previous actions although the arhat is already free of disturbing emotions. Much impressed by this clear and precise answer, the teacher called his student Togme (Asanga) from then on.

Gyalse Togme grew up to become an erudite scholar, but it was his tremendous loving-kindness and his embodiment of the mind of enlightenment *(bodhichitta)* that made him renowned as a true bodhisattva. As it is told in his life story, Gyalse Togme once made it his practice to bring food to a beggar who was tormented by a severe flea infection. One day the beggar was not at the place Gyalse usually found him. The master became worried and searched for him everywhere. Finally, he found him in a ditch, hiding from the scorn of the public. Feeling intense compassion, Gyalse Togme invited the destitute beggar to his room, where, having relieved him of his flea-infested clothes, he gave him food and drink and offered him a clean garment. When the beggar had gone, Gyalse Togme was left with the beggar's clothes—and plenty of fleas. Fearing that the fleas might die if he were to throw the clothes away, he decided to wear them, determined to nourish the fleas with his own blood. He gradually fell sick, and when a friend of Gyalse's visited, the friend discovered the cause of his disease and requested the master—for the sake of those benefited by his presence—to rid himself of the flea-infested clothes so that his precious life would not be endangered. Gyalse was unwilling to do so and remarked that in the past he had lost his life pointlessly countless times, whereas now he had the opportunity to make a valuable gift of his body. Miraculously, after he continued for several days to nourish the fleas with his blood, the fleas began to die naturally, without hatching any new eggs.

The stories of his life also tell of a time when his mere presence inspired a fox to stop hunting. It said that his being was of such a sensitive nature that he would often cry when he gave teachings. Because of this, Gyalse is at times contrasted with his contemporary, the renowned scholar Buton Rinchen Drub (1290–1364), who was famous for making his audience laugh.

## MODERN CONSIDERATIONS

MIND TRAINING is a powerful method for everyone who wishes for a change, for everyone who wishes to improve and transform their negative habitual tendencies and become a source of benefit and joy for themselves and others. Because of training sincerely and continuously in an unselfish altruistic attitude, many Kadam masters, including Gyalse Togme, could not bear the thought of taking birth in pure realms after death. They instead aspired to take birth in the hell realms to care for the sentient beings suffering there.

Some passages in the text, however, may require additional contextualization to become sensible to the modern reader. In particular, readers may feel put off by the passages in the text proclaiming that "women are a root of your negative emotions" and encouraging the practitioner to "give up the country of your birth and distance yourself from loved ones." How can a text that preaches the cultivation of compassion and the discernment of the ultimate view of reality espouse such views?

A transformation of the mind or a mere change of one's attitude is not something that happens suddenly, from one day to the next. It is a gradual process that, takes time. Beginners (and even some long-time practitioners) easily become distracted from this process by their habitual reliance on sensory pleasure. It is from this understanding that monks and full-time meditators (the traditional audience for Buddhist texts) are admonished to abandon female company. Nuns are similarly instructed to abandon male companions. There is nothing inherently holy about celibacy, but it can be a skillful means to help stabilize one's training and make the mind less afflicted and more workable.

For similar reasons, we are initially told to keep away from the place we conceive as our home, for in such a place our emotions of attachment and aversion abound. If we are continuously involved in feeding our negative emotions—our jealousy, anger, and self-pity—our practice is unlikely to develop. Therefore, the text admonishes us to initially gain some degree of emotional stability in a place of solitude before venturing back into situations where our negative emotions are likely to pop up continuously. Although such admonitions—staying away from the opposite sex or from the country of your birth— may sound uncompassionate and narrow-minded, they should be understood in their proper context: as preliminary instructions for a yogi who aspires to the ultimate goal of developing an unbiased feeling of loving-kindness and compassion toward all sentient beings.

A curious story tells how many of the old Kadam monasteries eventually became nunneries and illustrates some important points about mind training that should be kept in mind when reading *The Thiry-Seven Practices* and its commentary.[13] Once a *dakini*, a female emanation of enlightenment, came to one of the Kadam monasteries. The monks, who regarded discipline as paramount for their practice, immediately expelled her from the monastery's grounds. Upon receiving this welcome the dakini made a prediction that this practice of shunning women would, ironically, have the consequence that these monasteries would in the future be populated by nuns. We can interpret this story as a warning against a one-sided emphasis on formal discipline at the expense of the core of Mahayana thought, the mind of enlightenment. Most of the Kadam masters observed celibate vows, and they valued their code of monastic discipline highly, for the Kadam school was a reformist tradition that had among its objectives the restoration of the Vinaya tradition. However, this story tells us the importance of allowing one's practice to evolve progressively, just like the path laid out in this book.

While Chökyi Dragpa's initial chapters stress avoiding female company and places likely to cause feelings of attachment and aversion, it becomes clear from Chökyi Dragpa's subsequent discussion that practice does not simply end with this. The latter chapters in this book encourage us to see all phenomena as illusions and to understand their empty nature. They also explain how to bring painful circumstances—the experience of objects of aversion—as well as enjoyable circumstances—the experience of objects of attachment—onto the path through the force of compassion and insight. Thus, the bodhisattva must, as his or her practice develops, be able to skillfully remain in the midst of the most challenging situations by means of the power of insight united with compassion. *The Thirty-Seven Practices* guides us skillfully and gradually toward enlightenment, showing how as beginners, we avoid places or objects that might disturb our training while later, once our practice develops, we are encouraged as bodhisattvas to intentionally seek out these places or objects so that we may be able to actualize the training in qualities such as patience, impartial loving- kindness, and the recognition of the illusory nature of all phenomena.

## STRUCTURE OF THE TEXT

CHÖKYI DRAGPA'S COMMENTARY on *The Thirty-Seven Practices* exemplifies the diversity and richness of the Buddhist teachings. As its subtitle, *The Unity of Scriptures and Oral Instructions*, indicates, it applies a combination of two distinct features of the Buddhist tradition: classical scriptural statements and pithy oral instructions. Scripture includes two categories: the words of the Buddha as recorded in canonical texts *(bka' 'gyur)* as well as the explanations of these words as found in the classical Indian treatises *(bstan 'gyur)*. Concerning the latter of these two types of scripture, a genuine Buddhist treatise *(bstan bcos)* must possess two qualities: the capacity to cure the disease of the disturbing emotions, and the ability to protect beings from the infinite abyss of the lower realms of existence. The author of such a Buddhist treatise must also possess several qualifications. The foremost author is someone who has direct realization of the inherent nature of all things, but individuals without this fundamental realization may still compose a spiritual treatise if they have had a vision of their special deity and have been requested to write by that deity as well as by their teacher. A comprehensive knowledge of the whole field of Buddhist teaching is the minimum requirement for any author of a Dharma treatise. Chökyi Dragpa's explanations often cite and refer to these classical texts.

Oral instructions, the second type of teachings that Chökyi Dragpa draws upon, are condensations of the vast and profound meaning taught in the above-mentioned scriptures. Such oral instructions facilitate direct understanding and practical application. They are given by masters of the tradition by drawing directly upon their own practice experience to express the essence of practice. By receiving these instructions and incorporating them a practitioner may, without much previous study of scripture, arrive at the vital point of insight in a very short time. The language used in the oral instructions is often very blunt and down-to-earth, and we see the Kadam masters using folk sayings, stories, and analogies to explain the central messages of Buddhism. The subtitle of our commentary, *The Unity of Scriptures and Oral Instructions,* is the heart of the Kadam approach. The goal and basic identity of this tradition has been described as the realization that all Buddhist teaching and doctrine, in fact, are nothing but oral instruction.[14] Thus, through the Kadam approach one comes to see all classical scriptural statements as no different from the pithy oral instructions that are meant for direct, experiential application.

This is the understanding that Chökyi Dragpa works to convey to his reader. He explains this approach himself in a colophon toward the end of his commentary, but let me here briefly outline the structure of his explanation and the various elements it contains.

1) **Literal commentary.** Each root verse is followed by the commentator's clarification of the meaning of the specific verse. The emphasis here is on explaining, word for word, the statements of the root text.

2) **Scriptural statements.** Next Chökyi Dragpa supports his explanation of the verse by quoting words of the Buddha and passages from the treatises of great masters. By first bringing citations from sutras, he demonstrates that the words of the Enlightened One carry a primary importance. We can note a similar approach with regard to the treatises, where the commentaries composed by Indian masters are listed before those authored by Tibetans, thus showing respect for the origins of Buddhism in India. Hence, in almost all chapters, we see a number of sutra quotations followed by verses from the Indian master Shantideva's famed *Bodhicaryāvatāra (The Way of the Bodhisattva).* This beautiful presentation of bodhisattva conduct and view has been a major inspiration

for all mind training literature, and is enumerated among the "six basic texts of the Kadampas."[15]

3) **Instructions of the Kadam masters.** This section opens with words of Atisha. It is said that Atisha was unequalled in learning and renowned for his pure conduct and emphasis on the mind of enlightenment. Atisha's instructions are followed by quotes from his spiritual heirs, the great masters of the Kadam lineage.

4) **Additional instructions from Gyalse Togme.** Almost every chapter closes with a quote from "the bodhisattva himself," Gyalse Togme, whereby the explanation is brought back full circle to the author of *The Thirty-Seven Practices.*

Many of the scriptural citations and passages of Kadam instructions appear in the original Tibetan text in an abbreviated form, citing only an initial line with the expectation that the reader knows the remainder of the verse or passage by heart. For the sake of readers who are not quite as conversant in Buddhist literature as was the original audience of this text, I have added the missing lines in the English translation.

## ACKNOWLEDGMENTS

IT IS ONLY DUE TO the kindness, continuous support, instructions, and especially the living example of my perfect teacher Chökyi Nyima Rinpoche that I was able to translate this beautiful text into English.

This translation was begun many years ago, but I often put it aside because of the difficulties presented by some of the statements from the Kadampas. In my effort to understand these instructions, which were often written in a language no longer in use and at times in local dialects, I became a nuisance to many khenpos, continually requesting their help in deciphering these complex statements. It is not possible to mention here all of those who were kind enough to help me along the way, but first and foremost I would like to thank Khenpo Appe Rinpoche, whose kindness and vast knowledge touched my heart deeply. Furthermore, I would like to thank Dzogchen Khenpo Choga, Kyabje Khenpo Tashi Palden, Khenpo Pema Gyaltsen, Khenpo Sherab Sangpo, Lopon Yeshe Trinley, Lopon Sherab Oser, and Tulku Sangngag Tenzin for their kind explanations and assistance.

To Thomas Doctor, my husband, who compared the translation against the original, and to our families, I would like to extend my deepest gratitude for their continuous support and advice.

Moreover, I am very grateful to Kathy Morris for all her knowledgeable assistance and am extremely indebted to the skilled editor Joanne Larson for thoroughly editing this text and thereby improving it greatly. I would like to thank the experienced translator Erik Pema Kunsang for providing me with entries for my glossary. Thanks are also due to Dan Kaufer and Jonas Doctor for help with proofreading. Finally, I would like to extend my gratitude to Professor John Makransky for his kind encouragement and support, to David Kittelstrom for his experienced and perceptive advice, and to Wisdom Publications for making this text available to the public.

I sincerely regret any mistakes and mistranslations, which are solely due to my own shortcomings. It is my sincere hope and aspiration that this book, with its abundance of classical spiritual teachings and pithy, practical instructions, may inspire me and many other beings to develop the courage to let go of our usual selfish tendencies. May we embark on the challenging but truly enriching task of plowing the untilled field of our minds using the techniques that are here so beautifully shown.

*Heidi I. Köppl*

# INTRODUCTION

## BY CHÖKYI NYIMA RINPOCHE

IT IS SAID THAT THE BUDDHA, our teacher, has purified all negativity and perfected the potential for all positive qualities. What does that mean? To begin with, this statement makes us aware that Buddha is not some type of superman or extraterrestrial alien that just appeared on this earth endowed with superhuman qualities. We all possess the same potential that the Buddha possessed before becoming enlightened. Yet those positive qualities can only appear when the negative ones that cover them are eliminated. The Dharma, the teachings given by the Buddha, are based on his own personal experience and are concerned with nothing else than making our inherent positive qualities evident and our negative habitual tendencies diminish. The Dharma can guide us skillfully on a spiritual journey where we discover our real potential, previously unknown to us, and attain the same enlightened state as the Buddha himself.

Negativities, or obscurations, are mental defects, and our good qualities are positive mental factors. On a more subtle level, these mental defects can be divided into obscurations of negative emotions and cognitive obscurations. The obscurations of negative emotions include attachment, anger, and jealousy—all the coarse afflictive emotions. Cognitive obscurations include any conceptual thought that involves the ideas of subject, object, and action. When one has become free of the two obscurations and their habitual patterns, one is fully purified. This complete purification is indicated by the first syllable in the word *sang-gye*, the Tibetan term for Buddha. As for the second syllable, *gye*, it refers to the complete unfolding of countless qualities: wisdom, compassion, protective capacity, enlightened activity, and so forth. Someone who has achieved that level of perfection, a buddha, is a valid and authentic teacher.

Now that we have gained a glimpse of the meaning of buddha, we also need to understand the word *Dharma*. This refers to the teachings of the Buddha, which are both vast and profound. All of these teachings can, nevertheless, be condensed into oral instructions for practitioners—pith instructions that

directly target our mental defects, thereby accomplishing the central objective of all the Buddha's teachings. The commentary on *The Thirty-Seven
Practices* presented in this book is a perfect example of just such an oral instruction. Here we can, in a truly concise and efficient way, learn what the
spiritual path is like—how we can gradually dismantle our ingrown negative
habits, let go of our selfish concerns, and thus allow our intrinsically positive nature to shine through. Not confining our spiritual journey to four walls
and a meditation cushion, *The Thirty-Seven Practices* tells us how to deal con-
structively with the situations we encounter during all aspects of human life.
For instance, what can we do if we have hit an emotional rock bottom? How
should we react if we go bankrupt? What should we do when we are exceedingly happy, or when we become famous or very wealthy? Beneficial and
therapeutic reactions to criticism, slander, and abuse as well as to success,
popularity, and fame are described here, providing us with a great opportunity to progress on a challenging yet truly enriching journey in every moment. Not only is each verse followed by a clear and precise commentary,
the meaning of each verse is also clarified and elucidated by beautiful statements from the sutras and treatises. Last but not least, the unique abundance
of down-to-earth instructions of the Kadam masters, which often frankly
point at our personal shortcomings, are superb inspirations for our practice.
Without complicated terminology and in an immediately comprehensible
colloquial style, these pithy instructions can be easily remembered when we
face difficult situations.

In what follows, I have chosen to guide the reader into this wonderful
commentary through briefly commenting on *The Eight Stanzas of Mind Training*
by Langri Tangpa, which is a great example of the mind-training genre. You
might wonder why I have chosen this exact text. You might think that this introduction would be better served by commenting on the social and historical environment in which the commentary and its root text were composed.
On the one hand, I believe that it is indeed important to investigate the historical
and sociological context of an author and his text. However, I consider it to
be even more important to help the reader to open up right away to the essential quality of this commentary. It is for this purpose that I have chosen the
*Eight Stanzas* because of its stunningly practical, immediate, and self-trans-
forming approach. Although *The Thirty-Seven Practices* can be said to possess
many more different aspects and layers than the *Eight Stanzas*, nevertheless,
its essential quality comes down to nothing other than taming or turning
around our rigid egotistical mind in every moment. Hence, I have taken the

liberty here to directly point out this essential quality, which is so precisely and succinctly explained in *The Eight Stanzas of Mind Training*.

When reading both texts, we should try to assimilate their meaning into our own minds. We should not leave them as mere theory but should instead apply them to our lives. Remember the verses in all the different situations you meet during your daily life, and take them to heart as personal advice meant just for you.

The Dharma is taught so that it can be practically applied. The Dharma's objective can only be fulfilled if we *practice* it, so please keep in mind that the teachings are taught exclusively for the sake of personal application and practice. In order to apply the teachings, however, we need to know *how* to practice, which is explained in the oral instructions. When we receive oral instructions, we come to understand what practice means; it is then left up to us to simply apply our knowledge to our lives. If we apply the instructions the moment we hear them, then we will be able to observe some positive change right then and there. This is truly remarkable! Let us not leave these teachings as mere theoretical ramblings, for by causing the mind to become gentle and pliable, our practice will flourish in the same way as it did for countless masters of the past.

Among the many kinds of oral instructions, the instructions on mind training are especially important for us practitioners. We all need to tame our minds, to make them pliable and gentle. Unless we tame the rigid, wild character of our minds, our innate good qualities will not develop. So it is essential to learn the practice called mind training.

> *Considering that all sentient beings*
> *Accomplish a supreme purpose*
> *Superior to the wish-fulfilling jewel,*
> *I shall at all times hold them to be very precious.*

The first stanza says that I should consider all sentient beings to be precious. "I" refers to each one of us individually, and "all" includes all sentient beings, even down to the smallest insects. We should regard them all as precious regardless of whether they are enemies, friends, or strangers to us. We should do this with the thought that they accomplish a purpose that even surpasses what can be gained from a wish-fulfilling jewel. Many stories of ancient times tell of the existence of wish-fulfilling jewels that would grant all the wishes and fulfill all the hopes of anyone who supplicated them.

It is thanks to sentient beings that we can now practice the vast conduct of a bodhisattva—the six perfections of generosity, discipline, patience, diligence, meditative concentration, and wisdom, as well as the four means of magnetizing: being generous, speaking kind words, giving appropriate teachings, and maintaining consistency between one's words and actions. Practicing the six paramitas and four means of magnetizing leads us to enlightenment. Through these practices the bodhisattva comes to the aid of all sentient beings, despite their great number, despite any difficulties, and despite the great amount of time that may be required. In short, the vast conduct of a bodhisattva, so difficult to practice, is related to and dependent upon sentient beings.

If we wish to achieve perfect enlightenment, the benefit that we can receive from sentient beings far exceeds that granted by a wish-fulfilling jewel. A wish-fulfilling jewel may have the ability to dispel poverty, provide food or precious stones, or give us all the perfections and enjoyments of this present life, but it cannot give us supreme liberation.

The achievement of supreme liberation and the state of omniscience are indeed achieved by the kindness of sentient beings, who are limitless in number. For instance, being generous to sentient beings in the way of a bodhisattva enables us to gather the spiritual accumulations and purify our obscurations. Doing so, we will achieve perfect, supreme liberation, which is the greatest attainment of all. In that way, sentient beings grant something superior to anything a wish-fulfilling jewel could ever bestow.

Also, is it not taught that every sentient being has at some point throughout our countless lives been our kind parent? When they were our mother or our father, they cherished us with love and affection. Therefore, taking all this into account, we should at all times consider sentient beings to be dear and precious. We should not just care for them occasionally but cherish them continuously from the depth of our hearts with the affection of a mother for her only child.

> *When accompanying anyone anywhere,*
> *I must regard myself as the inferior to all*
> *And, from the core of my heart,*
> *Respectfully hold others as paramount.*

Whenever we are with others, we should, regardless of whether they may be considered inferior, equal, or superior to ourselves, always regard ourselves as inferior to them. With a sincere, heartfelt, and uncontrived determination, we should cherish others while perceiving them as our superiors. We should reflect on the great likelihood of their being more mature and evolved than we are in terms of intelligence and compassion. We should consider how it is very likely that they are capable and successful practitioners of the bodhisattva path, much better than we are at applying themselves to the practice of the paramitas. We should think that if we do not perceive their excellence and superiority, it must simply be due to our own delusions.

Our usual tendency is the complete opposite of this. We assume that we are better than others, and consequently, we regard others as inferior. Geshe Langri Tangpa instructs us to reverse this habitual tendency of regarding ourselves as superior, and in so doing he makes us aware that our usual attitude is extremely unwholesome and definitely not in tune with mind training. Therefore, in order to overcome our negative emotions such as pride and arrogance, we must sincerely believe from the core of our hearts that in terms of intelligence, compassion, and so forth, everyone is our superior and cherish them wholeheartedly.

> *In all activities may I examine my mind,*
> *And as soon as negative emotions arise,*
> *Since they cause trouble for myself and others,*
> *May I, Avert them, using direct methods.*

Whatever we may be doing—walking, sitting, eating, or lying down—we should always examine and analyze our mental state for negative emotions. As Dharma practitioners, we often have the tendency to divide the day into practice sessions and breaks. During our sessions we try to check on our mind, but during our breaks we behave the same as any worldly person, letting our mind be governed by all kinds of egoistic desires and negative emotions. But isn't our mind the main object of our practice? Because this mind is always with us, during our breaks and our sessions, we have the opportunity to practice all the time. Not only do we simply have the opportunity to practice, but as Dharma practitioners we are in fact required to maintain our practice continuously.

So what are we doing right now? Are we developing positive qualities such as loving-kindness or the insight into the empty nature of all phenomena? Or is the contrary the case—are we governed by negative emotions such as anger, stupidity, desire, and so on? Examine and work with your mind continuously in this way. We need to understand that negative emotions such as desire, anger, close-mindedness, pride, jealousy, and stinginess abound within us and that they are a danger to ourselves as well as others, causing both temporary and ultimate suffering. Therefore, the moment any negative emotion arises, we should immediately and without any hesitation avert it.

In the context of mind training, the self-cherishing attitude is specifically identified as the main culprit, the cause of all misery for oneself and others. Thus, as soon as we become aware that we are being selfish, we should immediately stop entertaining such egoistic desires and instead seek to cultivate the opposite—an altruistic attitude that is concerned with others' well-being. We should not wait, nor should we apply the antidote slowly. Realizing that such afflictive attitudes are poisonous, we must stop and destroy them, using direct methods, the very moment they appear.

If our aim is to be a true Dharma practitioner, then this is exactly the way to practice. In the teachings, negative emotions are compared to poison. But aren't negative emotions actually much more harmful than poison? Poison endangers our life; at worst we will die, causing this present life to end. However, negative emotions will not only bring suffering in this life but in all our lives to come. Moreover, they will not only cause pain to ourselves, they will bring pain and misery to many other sentient beings as well.

> *When seeing sentient beings of bad character*
> *Who are oppressed by fierce evil and suffering,*
> *May I cherish them, for this is as rare*
> *As the discovery of a precious treasure.*

All eight stanzas of this text instruct us in how to train our minds; they illustrate for us the vast conduct of a bodhisattva, which is directly opposite to our normal way of behaving. In this verse, for instance, we are encouraged to cherish beings of evil character by seeing them as more valuable than a precious treasure! Usually, when we meet somebody who is intensely angry, jealous, hateful, proud, arrogant, competitive, or mean, do we like that person? No, we will try our best to stay as far away as possible from such a nasty individual. The bodhisattva's orientation is completely different. First, a bodhisattva, when encountering sentient beings who are by nature angry, jealous, or proud, realizes that those beings are, in fact, suffering. He recognizes that such beings are oppressed and driven by extremely strong misery and evil. Not only have they accumulated numerous nonvirtuous actions throughout many past lives, they are continuing to do so in this life as well. In this way, their minds experience intense unhappiness, depression, and misery, which then manifests in their physical and verbal expression. They cannot really be blamed, for they are quite helpless; they are controlled by evil and suffering.

When meeting such beings, the bodhisattva wants to help. A bodhisattva will try his or her best to influence and establish a positive link with such a miserable person, either directly or indirectly. Let us try to do the same!

Moreover, it is said that we should consider such beings precious, that we should respond as if we had chanced upon a precious treasure. When finding a rare treasure, all that we wish for in terms of food, clothes, dwelling place, and so forth can be fulfilled, and all enjoyments and perfections of this life can be achieved. But discovering such a treasure is not an everyday event; it happens only rarely. Likewise, beings who are terribly oppressed by strong misery and evil are rare, and when meeting one we should acknowledge that we are now in a very special situation.

We should regard such people as our teachers. We can clearly recognize that their unpleasant behavior and the misery they experience stem from their own evil deeds and that this is what causes further suffering to themselves and others. When we understand the harm that nonvirtue brings to ourselves and others, we will be better able to train in the conduct of the bodhisattvas, and it will be easier for us to accomplish many challenging tasks. In relating with such difficult beings and in trying to help them, we have the perfect opportunity to gather the accumulations necessary for genuine spiritual progress and to purify our own obscurations. In this way we will, in the end, attain supreme liberation. So these beings of wicked character, driven by severe evil and suffering, are actually the perfect circumstance for attaining liberation and the state of omniscience. Once we have attained enlightenment, we will be able to accomplish the genuine welfare of sentient beings on a truly vast scale. Therefore, let us cherish these beings dearly.

This all sounds very beautiful, doesn't it? But you should understand that unless you really practice it, this instruction has no benefit.

> *When, out of jealousy, others*
> *Abuse and attack me in unjust ways,*
> *May I take the defeat upon myself*
> *And offer the victory to others.*

When out of strong envy, someone insults me directly or indirectly, treats me badly or attacks me, and so causes me pain, I will take this defeat or loss upon myself, thinking, "Whatever has happened must be my own fault. I was the one who committed all sorts of nonvirtuous deeds during my past lives, and as a result of that I am now mistreated and abused. So now I am clearing up my karmic debt—how wonderful!" This is the way we should accept this defeat.

When we get into such difficult situations, we must not retaliate and respond in the same way.

A bodhisattva trains in the "four virtuous practices": not responding with anger to those who are angry at you, not retaliating when beaten, not scolding in return when you are scolded, and not exposing the hidden faults of somebody who exposes your own. If we are fully able to train in these four virtuous practices, we will have embarked on the path of a bodhisattva. If we train in these practices, we will feel the beneficial results immediately. Not only we will feel the benefits, but also the aggressor will be indirectly benefited.

We will not have to wait long for situations to arise in which we'll have the opportunity to train in these four practices. We encounter such situations quite often, and so we are frequently in the fortunate position of being able to apply ourselves.

However, this practice is once again directly opposite to our normal inclinations. Usually, we happily accept victory and are eager to distribute any loss that we might experience to others. But here we are encouraged to turn this tendency around 100 percent: offer the victory to others and take any defeat upon yourself! For instance, when others insult us, they want to win the verbal combat, hoping for some good feelings as a reward. Therefore, we should offer them all victory and profit. Fundamentally, this means that we think, "May any victory, gain, and happiness—in short, everything good—ripen upon sentient beings, and may everything unpleasant that can be experienced fall only upon me."

> *Even if one whom I have helped*
> *And in whom I have great hopes*
> *Instead irrationally causes me harm,*
> *May I regard that one as my genuine spiritual teacher.*

There may be someone for whom we have great hopes and expectations—someone we have helped in the past by supplying food, clothes, a house, education, and so forth, and who we now expect will do good. With complete disregard for ourselves, we have put all our efforts into making that person truly successful. However, all the while we have also entertained subtle selfish thoughts such as, "Since I am truly kind to this person, he or she will certainly return my kindness in the future." What if that person now not only abstains from benefiting me and disregards my kindness, but on top of that, in a way that is absurdly unjustified, begins to spend all his energy on bringing me physical or mental pain? How would we feel? Certainly, our tendency would be to suffer deeply—to feel terribly hurt, shocked, and even aggressive. Yet here we are instructed to regard this person as our sacred spiritual teacher. Why? It is he or she who makes us train in the practice of a bodhisattva and who grants us a perfect opportunity to accomplish it. Is it not this person who exposes and makes us aware of our own selfish interests? When I cared for this person so dearly, I kept certain expectations in mind. Did I not hope for at least some kind of reward? Such expectations are of an entirely selfish nature, and it is thanks to this person that I have now become aware of my own selfish character. Such self-centered interests are the root of all misery, and now, finally, I am able to identify and seize this culprit who has been lying unnoticed behind all my thoughts and actions. Having now identified the root of my trouble, I am able to overcome and eliminate it. Therefore, without feeling the slightest anger against this person, we should regard him or her as our sacred spiritual friend, who grants us such supreme insight and gives us the opportunity to practice the conduct of a bodhisattva.

> *In short, may I offer to all my mothers,*
> *Both directly and indirectly, all happiness and benefit,*
> *And may I secretly take upon myself*
> *All the harms and sufferings of my mothers.*

This verse summarizes all the previous verses in just a few lines, telling us to give all happiness and benefit to our mothers. There is no doubt that all sentient beings have been our kind parents in the past. Since there is no sentient being who has not been our loving mother in the past, let us offer them any amount of happiness and benefit we can, both directly and indirectly, and let us do so without any bias or partiality. With an abundance of methods, may we make them happy, even if it is only temporarily, and may we finally grant them the gift of ultimate happiness, the state of liberation! Let us secretly take upon ourselves, without making it known to anybody, whatever harm and misery our mothers may experience. May we be able to ease their pain and do away with all their misery. How can we feel well and comfortable if all our kind parents are suffering? By all means we must take their suffering and pain upon ourselves. And why should we do this secretly? If we do it this way, we will not fall into the trap of arrogance, and we will be able to overcome our pride.

*All of that must not be polluted*
*By the stains of the eight concerns.*
*By understanding all phenomena as illusion,*
*May we be free from the fetters of attachment.*

May these practices of training our minds—such as granting victory, happiness, and benefit to others and taking loss, blame, and harm upon ourselves—not be tainted by the eight worldly concerns. These are the wish for gain, happiness, fame, and praise, and the desire to avoid their opposites. What usually happens when we are praised, become famous, are happy, and manage to get wealthy? We become exhilarated. But when the opposite happens—if we experience any kind of loss, pain, or abuse or if we are ignored or become infamous—we tend to become badly depressed. Here we are instructed not to get involved with these mundane and selfish inclinations but to remain completely unpolluted by such mundane concepts when training our minds.

Indirectly, we are also advised not to be pretentious and insincere regarding our Dharma practice. We might start to feel that the outer form of being a Dharma practitioner is very important and begin to put more emphasis on our outer "Dharma appearance" than on our actual mental state. How can we avoid practicing in an insincere, pretentious way? If we allow these instructions to touch our hearts, pretentiousness and superficiality will automatically be cleared away.

Beyond remaining uninvolved in the eight mundane concerns, we must also understand that all phenomena are actually illusions. Whatever we do, all our practices must be embraced by an insight into the empty nature of all phenomena. Through understanding that all phenomena are unreal, insubstantial, illusory, and nothing but the expression of emptiness, we become liberated from all fetters of grasping. It is because of grasping that we circle in the three realms of existence and experience myriad miseries. Therefore, may we be freed from the bondage of attachment by actualizing the correct view of the nature of all phenomena: simplicity, free of all mental constructs. In this way may we perfect the welfare of all beings, without any attachments, fixations, or preferences. This is the perfect way of practice!

Again, when studying such stanzas, it is important not to leave them as mere theory but to actually apply them to one's state of being. These are just a few lines, and they are quite easy to understand. Nevertheless, what they address is extremely profound. If we really persevere, we can put into practice these instructions in which all the meanings of sutras and treatises are complete.

To train our minds is so very important! If we fail to train and purify our mind, it will be just like an uncultivated field where no seeds can grow. A field must be ploughed and carefully prepared so that it has the correct level of moisture, fertilizer, and so forth. Likewise, our minds must be cultivated. An extremely efficient way to make this happen is the practice of mind training. When our minds have been cultivated through the practice of mind training, all higher practices will occur spontaneously. Compassion will increase on its own and insight will naturally unfold.

The heart, root, and center of all Buddhist practices is the unity of compassion and emptiness. This unity is indispensable. For our practice, just this unity alone is all that we need; without it everything is lacking. Whoever knows this unity will reach liberation, the state of omniscience. On the other hand, one may be very learned in the scriptures, perform numerous practices, and go through millions of recitations and visualizations, yet if one fails to understand this unity, one will not travel far. It will be impossible for true realization to arise. This unity of compassion and emptiness is of utmost importance. And for the realization of this unity to genuinely take place we must train our minds. Without mind training, we will never really understand emptiness and compassion.

Since training the mind is very important, I encourage you all to study and practice this. In particular, we should all read these teachings in order to apply them directly to our minds. As we apply them, we must continuously check our minds. "Three days have now passed since I started to practice mind training. What has happened? What's new about my mind?" "It's been a week since I started practicing mind training. How is my mind; is it different?" "A month has now passed…six months…a year. How is my mental state different than it was a month ago…a year ago?" We should analyze our minds in this way and educate ourselves.

When training their minds in this way, the Kadam masters of the past would sit near two piles of stones—black stones to their right and white stones to their left. Carefully observing their minds, they would pick up a white stone and place it in front of them whenever they had a virtuous thought, and they would place a black stone in front of them for each nonvirtuous thought. In the beginning, after a long day of practice, they would end up with a mountain of black stones and only two or three white stones. After counting the stones they would scold themselves, saying what bad practitioners they were, giving rise to only nonvirtuous thoughts and never bringing forth any virtuous ones. Continuing to practice in this way, after some time they would end up with equal numbers of black and white stones, at which point they would tell themselves, "Now I am not that bad anymore, but nevertheless, I am still far from being a good practitioner."Finally, at the end of each day there would be many white stones and only a few black ones. Upon seeing this, they would praise themselves, saying, "Today you finally managed to train your mind well."

There are plenty of such stories of how the past Kadam masters trained their minds. We should follow their example; merely reading their life stories or their teachings is not enough. We really have to apply these instructions experientially. If we fail to take the teachings to heart, we will not be able to accomplish anything. So please take these teachings seriously and apply them to your minds.

# THE EXCELLENT VASE
# OF NECTAR

*The Unity of Scriptures and Oral Instructions*

*A Commentary on Gyalse Togme's*

The Thirty-Seven Practices of a Bodhisattva

**BY CHÖKYI DRAGPA**

*Namo Guru*

These aggregates, the illusory bodies of myself and others,
If sick, how enjoyable their sickness!
This is the exhaustion of bad karma, gathered in the past.
The various activities of one's Dharma practice
Exist for the purpose of purifying the two obscurations.

If not sick, how enjoyable that is!
When body and mind are well, virtuous activity increases.
To engage in virtue with body, speech, and mind
Is the fulfillment of this human birth.

If lacking riches, how enjoyable that is!
Uninvolved with protecting and unconcerned about losing.
Disturbances arising from conflicts, however many there may be,
Surely occur because of wealth, cherished and desired.

If wealthy, how enjoyable that is!
Let the virtuous gathering of merit increase.
Immediate and future benefits and happiness, however many there
    may be,
Are certainly the fruition of merit.

If dying soon, how enjoyable that will be!
Unobstructed by bad circumstances and
Aided by one's excellent habits at the meeting point,
One is certain to enter the unmistaken path.

If living long, how enjoyable that is!
Bringing forth the harvest of experience.
Without letting the moisture of the oral instructions evaporate,
Sustaining them at length, they will grow to fullness.
Whatever may come, meditate on it as being enjoyable.

This was spoken in response to a geshe's questions as to what should be done
when one falls sick. This way of taking sickness and so forth onto the path was
arranged by the monk Togme, who teaches the Dharma.

May it be virtuous!
*Mangalam.*

# THE GOODNESS
# OF THE BEGINNING

I bow to the great heroes and their children,
Those who have arrived and those who will arrive at the great
    realization,
Bearing with great courage their burden to guide to great
    enlightenment
All beings extending throughout space.

He who with his eyes of great compassion
Never shirks his promise to gaze on those who wander,
To the Dharma lord who is the display of this supremely noble one,
To the feet of Gyalse Togme, devoutly I bow.

The supreme entrance gate through which all the victors and their
    children,
As many as there are, have passed or will pass,
That excellent path that takes one from bliss to bliss,
Its practice I will here explain, delivering it into your hand.

There are three points to the explanation of the practices of the bodhisattvas,
composed by the glorious son of the victorious ones, Gyalse Togme.

    1. Praise and promise to compose
    2. The nature of the treatise to be composed
    3. The meaning of the conclusion

## PRAISE

*Namo Lokeshvaraya*
*Seeing that all phenomena are beyond coming or going,*
*He strives solely for the benefit of sentient beings.*

*To the supreme master and protector, Avalokiteshvara,*
*I prostrate continuously and respectfully with body, speech, and mind.*

As for the first of these points, "Namo Lokeshvaraya" means "Prostrations to the lord of the world." His omniscient wisdom sees all phenomena as the natural state, exactly as it is, in which the complexities of any of the eight extremes—coming and going, permanence and nihilism, existence and no existence, one and many—have not the slightest bearing. Yet, by the power of great compassion and love, he strives one-pointedly for the welfare of sentient beings. To this supreme lama who shows me the path of the Great Vehicle and who is inseparable from the noble Avalokiteshvara, the personification of the compassion of all the buddhas, the protector of all those who are without protection, I prostrate continuously with respectful body, speech, and mind.

## THE PROMISE TO COMPOSE

*The perfectly enlightened ones, sources of benefit and happiness,*
*Appear from having accomplished the holy Dharma.*
*Since that accomplishment depends on knowing the practices,*
*I will here explain the practice of the bodhisattvas.*

The perfectly enlightened ones, those who have become the sources of temporary benefit and ultimate bliss, from what cause did they appear? In the context of training on the path, they appeared solely from having practiced the holy Dharma of the Great Vehicle in a correct manner. You may then ask, "How is that?" At the very outset, they bring forth a mind that is basically great compassion. Thereafter, they gather the accumulations, which are comprised of the six paramitas—the aspect of means, generosity, and so forth—as well as the aspect of knowledge that realizes all phenomena to be without self-nature. All such qualities depend exclusively on knowing how to practice. Therefore, for those who wish to train on the path of the Great Vehicle in order to achieve buddhahood, the following promise is made: "I shall explain the training in the motivation and conduct of the bodhisattvas, just as it appears in the *pitakas* of the Great Vehicle and in the commentaries on their intent." Furthermore, from *The Enlightenment of Vairochana:*

Lord of Secrets, the omniscient wisdom arises from the root of compassion, appears from its cause, which is bodhichitta, and is perfected through skillful means.

From *Precious Garland of the Middle Way:*

When I myself and the whole world
Aspire to attain unsurpassable enlightenment,
Its root is the mind of enlightenment, as stable as Mount Meru,
Compassion that pervades in all directions
And wisdom not dependent upon duality.

As to the reason why this great being, Gyalse Togme, is capable of explaining the practice of the bodhisattvas to others, the qualifications for composing such a treatise are complete since he relied upon numerous teachers, became learned in the oceanlike Mahayana scriptures, beheld the face of his special deity, and so forth. In particular, he is capable because, as is described in his life story, he himself trained in all aspects of the conduct of the bodhisattvas in a correct manner.

## THE NATURE OF THE TREATISE TO BE COMPOSED

As to the second point, the nature of the treatise, there are two parts:

Part 1: The preliminaries, the manner of entering into the Dharma
Part 2: The main part, demonstrating the paths of the three kinds of beings

The first part is divided in terms of seven points.

# THE PRELIMINARIES

*The Manner of Entering into the Dharma*

1

# MAKING THE FREEDOMS AND
# RICHES MEANINGFUL

FIRST, AS TO making the freedoms and riches, which are difficult to obtain, meaningful:

> *At this time of having obtained the rare great ship of freedoms and riches,*
> *Without any distraction day and night,*
> *In order to liberate oneself and others from the ocean of samsara*
> *Is the practice of the bodhisattvas.*

The support of a human body endowed with the eight freedoms and complete with the ten riches resembles a great ship. "The eight freedoms" means not being born in any of the eight unfree states. "The ten riches" consist of the five intrinsic ones (so called because these are conducive circumstances for Dharma practice that must be complete within oneself), as well as of the five extrinsic ones (so called because these are conducive circumstances that must be complete from outside oneself).

The difficulty of obtaining such a human body can be demonstrated through example, enumeration, and cause.[16]

Through this attainment the great objectives of liberation and omniscience can be accomplished. Therefore, when it is obtained, one should not let this support go to waste through engaging in pointless and trivial objectives. Rather, in order to liberate oneself and others from the immense ocean of samsara, one should listen to the oral instructions of a spiritual friend of the Great Vehicle. Moreover, one should reflect upon the meaning of these instructions and analyze them by means of the four kinds of reasoning. Finally, one must meditate by correctly bringing the instructions to mind. This process should be engaged in at all times, without any distraction, day and night. Such is the practice whereby all bodhisattvas make the freedoms and riches meaningful.

Furthermore, from the *Sutra of the Ornamental Array*:

> Becoming a human being is a difficult attainment;
> Attaining the perfectly pure freedoms is even more difficult.

From *The Way of the Bodhisattva*:

> The freedoms and riches are extremely difficult to obtain;
> They accomplish the purpose of human existence.

Further:

> Based on the ship, the human body,
> One becomes liberated from the great river of suffering.

*Letter to a Friend* states:

> Since it is extremely difficult to obtain a human birth,
> By practicing the holy Dharma, lord of humans, make it meaningful!

Further, the words "freedoms and riches" are the presentations of the freedoms and riches as essential qualities. The words "the great ship" and "in order to liberate oneself and others from the ocean of samsara" indicate the great purpose of the freedoms and riches. As to what beings wish for, it is the truly elevated life of a god and human being, the definitive good of liberation, or the supreme definitive good of omniscience. Whatever one wants to accomplish, one can do so by means of this support.

As for the phrase "rare," its rarity is demonstrated by means of example, enumeration, and cause.

Phrases such as "without distraction day and night" and "to listen, reflect, and meditate" point out that one needs to strive in the Dharma in order to take full advantage of that which one has obtained.

Though the root text does not mention the difficulty of obtaining such a support in the future if one does not endeavor in it now, *The Way of the Bodhisattva* says the following:

> If one does not accomplish its purpose in this life,
> This ship will be difficult to find in the future.

Furthermore, from the unequaled great Lord Atisha:

> The body of perfect freedoms and riches,
> Difficult to obtain, has been obtained;

Since it will be extremely difficult to obtain in the future,
By persisting in practice, it should now be made meaningful!

Dromtonpa also said:

This support, with its freedoms and riches,
Is exceedingly difficult to obtain.
It is so rare to encounter the teachings of Lord Buddha;
Hence, you must not waste the freedoms and riches, so difficult to
obtain!

Dromtonpa once asked Chen-ngawa: "Do you contemplate the attainment of the human body with its freedoms and riches?" Chen-ngawa answered: "When I think about the difficulty of obtaining the freedoms and riches, I find no time for sleep and leisure." This is what he said, and the accounts state that he remained exclusively in meditation. When alternating between his practices, he recited:

If, when free and enjoying conducive circumstances,
One does not take firm hold of oneself,
One falls into the abyss and becomes dependent.
How then can one ever rise again?[17]

Having said that, he meditated.

Puchungwa explains the following:

Having obtained the body of freedoms and riches, if one dies without having been virtuous, it's like finding a priceless jewel and throwing it away without ever having enjoyed it. On the contrary, if one does evil, it's like exchanging a jewel for a piece of rotten food mixed with poison.

Potowa states:

Without letting these freedoms and riches, so difficult to attain and so easy to destroy, go to waste, you must now give them meaning and make them perfect!

Kharagpa explains:

> When this precious human body with its freedoms and riches,
> So difficult to obtain, is attained,
> Then without letting this attainment fade away,
> It should be made a perpetual harvest.

Moreover, he also uses the image of taking the support of the human body as if it were a ship.

Shabopa says:

> Presently, we have obtained a human body with its freedoms and riches, met a spiritual teacher, and connected with the Mahayana teachings. Now, at this very time, we must prepare for our future lives and get a firm footing in the direction of liberation and omniscience.

Furthermore, the precious Dharma lord Gyalse Togme states the following:

> Since the freedoms and riches are so difficult to acquire, when you obtain them, make them meaningful.

He continues in this way:

> Therefore, learned ones, without deceiving yourselves,
> Practice the sacred Dharma correctly,
> Through authentically combining listening, reflecting, and
>     meditating;
> Thus, make these freedoms and riches a meaningful gain!

He also practiced this way himself.

# 2

## GIVING UP YOUR HOME

CONCERNING GIVING UP your home, the source of the three poisons:

> *Toward friends, attachment rages like a river;*
> *Toward enemies, hatred blazes like fire.*
> *Therefore, it is the practice of bodhisattvas to give up that home,*
> *Where the darkness of stupidity, of forgetting what to accept and reject,*
>   *prevails.*

If you stay in your homeland and try to practice the Dharma, your focus will naturally return to beloved ones—your parents, due to mutual deep affection, and companions, due to attachment, and so forth. Hence, desirous attachment, raging like a river, will arise and carry one away in the stream of existence. Similarly, the strong aversion felt toward enemies causes anger to burn like fire, scorching the virtuous accumulations of oneself and others. A dense, dark stupidity arises within oneself and will cause the mindfulness that correctly accepts the virtues, which are to be adopted, and rejects the nonvirtues, which are to be abandoned, to degenerate and be forgotten. Therefore, to give up that homeland that naturally brings about an abundance of faults is the practice of all bodhisattvas—their way of abandoning an unwholesome place, which is the root of attachment and aversion.

Furthermore, from the *Sutra Inspiring Supreme Intention*:

> It is best to go a hundred miles away
> From wherever there is entanglement and arguing;
> Don't remain and reside for even an instant
> Where negative emotions prevail.

If one resides in one's homeland—a place that is a source of defects such as attachment and aversion, entanglements and arguments—one will fall under the power of negative emotions and be unable to practice the Dharma. Therefore, it is taught that one must leave that place behind. In particular, "leaving one's home to become a homeless renunciate" means: Having left behind all those friends who are the basis for the arising of attachment and also those enemies who are the objects of one's anger, one should follow in the footsteps of the Buddha.

From the same sutra:

> For what purpose do these entanglements arise?
> You own no field and likewise no business;
> You have no wife, no sons, no daughters,
> No household, and not even a gathering of friends;
> You have neither servants, maids, nor master.
> Once you become ordained, don't engage in dispute!

Likewise, concerning the necessity of giving up friends, *The Way of the Bodhisattva* states:

> Beings who are themselves impermanent
> Are greatly attached to that which is also passing.

From the *Jataka Stories* comes the following:

> If you practice the Dharma, escape from your household business.
> How can one possibly practice the Dharma if inclined toward a household?

Through these and other quotations, the faults of remaining at home and the benefits of becoming a renunciate are extensively taught.

To be a renunciate, you must be like the deer and the birds, without considering anything whatsoever—country, friends, place, or livelihood—as your own. The *Moon Lamp Sutra* states the following:

> Those who regard nothing as their own
> And who have never had a master of any kind,
> Who remain like a rhinoceros in this world—
> They are like the wind moving through the sky.

If, after giving up one's homeland, one still remains among people and falls under the power of attachment and aversion, that contradicts the Dharma.

Furthermore, the single god, Lord Atisha, said:

> Demolish that demonic prison, your homeland!
> Cut through the ties of worldly concerns!

> Your beloved friend and hated enemy,
> Evil actions, the land of attachment and aversion, escape from it all!

He continued:

> Keep far away from places harmful for your mind;
> Stay at a place where your virtue always increases!

Dromtonpa states the following:

> Thoroughly cut off the samsara of your cherished evil country!

And:

> Rely entirely on an abode free from attachment and aversion!

In Potowa's teachings one finds statements such as:

> Give up the country of your birth and distance yourself from
> loved ones!

And:

> Move always like the sun and the moon, not keeping to one place
> or settling down in one land!

Moreover, he said that although the three abandonments—forsaking your birthplace, severing connections with loved ones, and giving up unexamined objects[18]—are the oral tradition of Radreng, all future generations will have a hard time practicing these three.

Kharagpa explains:

> Giving up the three things means: there is the giving up of the
> country one was born in; the giving up of one's home and house-
> hold; and the giving up of works and pursuits.

Furthermore, Gyalse Togme himself said:

> After giving up attachment to your country, the source of faults,
> Stay in a place where your virtue increases!

Following *The Way of the Bodhisattva*, he taught extensively on how, when practicing the path of the Great Vehicle, one needs to give up a place that creates attachment and aversion, and in his own practices he acted accordingly.

# 3

# ADHERING TO SOLITUDE

CONCERNING ADHERING to solitude, the source of good qualities:

> *Abandoning negative places, disturbing emotions gradually subside;*
> *Being free from distraction, the practice of virtue spontaneously increases;*
> *With brightened awareness one feels confidence in the Dharma;*
> *To adhere to solitude is the practice of the bodhisattvas.*

After one has given up a negative area, such as one's homeland, one needs to adhere to solitude. By doing so, all negative emotions, such as attachment and aversion, will gradually subside and diminish, causing one's discipline to become pure. Since secluded places are devoid of the faults of distractions and business—that is, such obligations as merchandising or working in the fields for the sake of friends, family, oneself, and others—the virtuous training of the three doors, such as exertion in the yoga of one-pointed absorption, will spontaneously increase. By attaining mental abiding, one's mind becomes pliable. Through intelligently investigating and analyzing the meaning of the sacred Dharma with this bright awareness, certainty arises, one is better able to practice, and the three kinds of training[19] will develop. Adhering to solitude endowed with many such qualities is the practice of bodhisattvas—their way of adhering to a conducive environment.

Furthermore, from *Ornament of the Sutras*:

> The place where intelligent ones practice
> Is well supplied, an excellent dwelling place,
> An excellent soil, endowed with good companions,
> And graced by yogic bliss.

An excellent dwelling place is one where the supplies of alms and so forth are plentiful and where there are no robbers or thieves. Excellent soil is soil where no diseases caused by the five elements arise and where excellent companions in harmony with the Dharma abide. It is a place graced with the qualities of yogic bliss, since there are no hindrances to meditative absorption. One must stay in such a place.

*Letter to a Friend* states the following:

> One remains in a place that is conducive and relies on holy beings.

From *The Way of the Bodhisattva*:

> In that way, become disenchanted with the objects of your desires;
> Engender fondness for solitude
> In the midst of a peaceful forest
> Empty of arguing and negative emotions.

Having become disenchanted with the shortcomings of distraction and business and having left them far behind, one must practice the Dharma in solitude endowed with good qualities. But how does one practice? Concerning this, the same source says:

> Recalling the qualities of solitude,
> Pacify thinking and meditate on bodhichitta.

It is said that one needs to meditate upon compassionate love and bodhichitta, whereby one exchanges oneself for others. In the same way, the *Supreme Jeweled Cloud Sutra* and the *Sutra Requested by the Householder Ugra* explain that, while abiding in solitude, one must engage solely in virtue.

Concerning the qualities of remaining in solitude, the *Moon Lamp Sutra* teaches extensively about the qualities and benefits. For instance:

> The qualities of abiding in solitude
> Are constant renunciation toward the conditioned,
> Not the slightest desire toward anything worldly,
> And not the slightest increase in any of the defilements.

Moreover, Lord Atisha proclaimed:

> Until you have reached stability, business will be harmful.
> Therefore, take to a deep forest for solitude.

In his *Method for Accomplishing the Path of the Mahayana* he teaches in the same way. Atisha continues:

> This is not the time to take up a retinue;
> This is the time to rely on solitude!

Along with:

> Having stayed in solitude, one must come to give up the desires and concerns of this life, solely practicing the Dharma, for one should be without regrets at the time of death.

Dromtonpa explains:

> This present time of degeneration is not a time when ordinary beings to actually benefit sentient beings without having first trained their minds, by remaining in solitude, in the bodhichitta of love and compassion.

Potowa said:

> Staying in solitude is the cause for samadhi to increase and also the cause for discipline to become pure.

Neuzurpa claims the following:

> While relying on solitude, correctly accepting and rejecting virtue and evil, if one then diminishes one's activities, the Dharma will be accomplished.

Geshe Nambarwa states:

> Without having trained the inner mind, your kindhearted intentions cannot remain stable. Therefore, cultivate the mind of enlightenment in solitude.

Furthermore, the great Gyalse Togme himself says:

> Relinquishing attachment toward friends, enemies, enjoyments, and
>     dear ones,
> One should ceaselessly meditate on the mind of enlightenment
> In a supreme place of solitude
> So that all beings, equal to the sky, may be established in happiness.

He taught so repeatedly and applied it in his own practice as well.

4

# GIVING UP CONCERN
# FOR THIS LIFE

REGARDING GIVING UP concern for this life through remembering impermanence:

> *Separated from each and every long-acquainted companion,*
> *Leaving behind hard-earned wealth and possessions,*
> *Guest-like consciousness abandons its guesthouse, the body;*
> *To give up concern for this life is the practice of the bodhisattvas.*

Regardless of how many friends and loved ones, such as our parents, we may have, even those who have long accompanied us and with whom we have even spent our entire lives, at the moment of death, will either abandon us or we will abandon them. It is certain that we will become separated from each other.

Our possessions and wealth that we, undaunted by evil and suffering, have struggled to amass by means of great hardship cannot be carried with us at the point of death; not even the tiniest scrap can follow us.

While the mind refuses to let go, still, leaving everything behind, it departs like a hair plucked from a block of butter. Not only that, this guesthouse of a body, which has always accompanied us and which is concocted of a mass of flesh and bones, will be flung away by its guest-like consciousness as we depart alone and friendless for an unknown destination. Thus, one reflects on all aspects of departure from this life.

From the present day onward, give up concern for all the activities of this life; they abound with shortcomings and triviality such as vanquishing enemies, catering to friends, and cultivating fields. Instead, give rise to a mind that strives for the sake of the next life and beyond. In this way, one enters the Dharma. Such is the practice of bodhisattvas whereby they cast off concern for this life.

Furthermore, from a sutra:

> The three realms are impermanent like autumn clouds;
> Seeing the birth and death of beings is like watching a drama.

There are numerous other examples, which all show that the outer vessel and its inner contents are impermanent.

Likewise, from the *Jataka Stories*:

> From that point when one first enters the womb,
> All worldly beings, having entered that path
> Will, without straying onto another path,
> Come ever closer to the Lord of Death.

From *The Way of the Bodhisattva*:

> Caught by the net of negative emotions,
> Entangled in the trap of rebirth,
> Yet I am still not aware
> That I have strayed into the mouth of the Lord of Death.

Since whoever at the outset is born is also not beyond death in the end, one should make "remembrance of death" one's contemplation. Though there are many different approaches to contemplation, here the contemplation of the three roots, the nine reasons, and the three decisions will be explained. The three roots are the following:

1. Death is certain.
2. When we will die is uncertain.
3. At the point of death, nothing other than Dharma is of benefit.

As for the first root, the certainty of death, there are three explanations:

> In the past no one has ever remained, never to die.
> The physical body is conditioned.
> Life is being depleted with each instant.

Concerning the second, the uncertainty of the time of death:

> The life span is uncertain.
> The body lacks any core.
> Circumstances conducive to death are plentiful.

Concerning the third, the failure of anything other than the Dharma to benefit at the point of death:

> Friends will be of no benefit.
> Food and wealth will be of no benefit.
> Even one's body will be of no benefit.

All these points establish the certainty of death and so forth. Without elaborating on each of these extensively, the last three reasons are explicitly identified in the root verse.

Moreover:

Since it is certain that one will die, one decides on the need to practice the Dharma so that there will be definite benefit at the point of death.

Since the time of death is uncertain, one decides on the need to practice the Dharma from the present moment on.

Since nothing whatsoever other than the Dharma is of benefit, one decides on the need to practice solely the Dharma.

*The Way of the Bodhisattva* states the following:

> Forsaking everything, one must depart;
> But because of not understanding that,
> I have done so much evil
> For the sake of friends and foes.

That shows the fault of not contemplating death.

From a sutra:

> Of all the ploughing, the autumn ploughing is the best.[20]

Thus, if we become involved with the fantasies of this life, whatever goodness we create will not turn into the genuine, divine Dharma but instead will become a mere reflection of it. Therefore, we should not get involved in that way.

It is taught that the extraordinary direct cause for cutting through fantasies regarding this life is precisely this contemplation on death.

Moreover, Lord Atisha stated the following:

> Casting everything behind, you must depart. Therefore, give up
> all pursuits and be without attachment toward anything.

Dromtonpa explains:

Life is fleeting. Like a flash of lightning illuminating the sky,
It is a phenomenon that perishes as soon as it occurs.

And:

If we don't give up thoughts of this life, then whatever we do will
not become the Dharma, since it will not be beyond the eight
worldly concerns. But if we have given up thoughts of this life,
we will walk on the path of liberation, without involvement in
the eight worldly concerns.

Yerba Shangtsun states:

In order to discard the desires of this life it is important to continually contemplate their remedy—impermanence. If one does
not give rise to the thought of impermanence in the early morning, then by noon all of one's activities will have been for the sake
of this life alone. If one doesn't give rise to the thought of impermanence at noon, then in the afternoon all will have been done
for this life alone. If all concerns have been for this life, none of your
deeds have become the Dharma.

Chen-ngawa relates:

Without a practice session on impermanence in the morning, the
whole day will be exclusively occupied with the concerns of
this life.

Kharagpa says the following:

There is no place where people remain without dying;
Death is certain and soon we will die.
Since nothing is of benefit when dying,
Take to heart that there is no time to waste.

Dragyabpa states:

However much effort, invoked through concern for this life, you
may have applied, when you die tomorrow you must leave naked
and empty-handed. Therefore, before death approaches, you
should practice a Dharma that is not mixed with concern for
this life.

Kamapa explains:

> Death ought to make us fearful right now,
> For we mustn't quake in fear on the verge of dying.
> We do the opposite; we're presently fearless,
> Yet, on the verge of passing away, we will claw our chests with our
>     fingernails.

Neuzurpa comments:

> There are three things that occur simultaneously: the first is that
> one recalls one's own mortality; the second is that one gives up
> concern for this life; and the third is that one practices the Dharma.
> Thinking that one will not die, having great concern for this life,
> and doing evil are also three things that occur simultaneously.

These are the benefits of contemplating death and the faults of not contemplating it.

Furthermore, there are many statements by various holy beings describing
how remembering impermanence is of utmost importance, since it first acts
as a cause for entering the Dharma, next enhances our diligence, and finally helps
us to attain the luminous *dharmakaya*.

Moreover, from Gyalse Togme himself:

> If an unfabricated feeling of impermanence arises, then under no
> circumstances will one be able to think of anything that isn't the
> Dharma. There are very few practitioners who give rise to this ex-
> perience authentically.

And:

> Death is certain, but the time of death is uncertain.
> At the time of death, the Dharma is sure to benefit.

He made many such statements and, in addition, took this as his main
practice.

5

GIVING UP BAD COMPANY

REGARDING GIVING UP the adverse circumstance of bad company:

> *If, while befriending someone, the three poisons increase,*
> *The activities of study, reflection, and meditation degenerate,*
> *And love and compassion disappear,*
> *Then it is the practice of the bodhisattvas to give up this bad company.*

When we are in the company of certain friends, our negative emotions, the three poisons that cause the life force of liberation to be cut, may increase. Meanwhile, the activities of the sacred Dharma, such as study, reflection, and meditation, which are the main cause for accomplishing liberation, may automatically degenerate. Moreover, base company might cause all the virtuous qualities accumulated within us throughout the past, such as the very roots of the Mahayana path—bodhichitta, love, and compassion—to completely disappear. To abandon all such immoral acquaintances and unwholesome friends, conceiving of them as dangerous wild animals, is the practice of all bodhisattvas—their manner of giving up bad company.

From *Purposeful Expressions*:

> Don't associate with people who are influenced by evil.
> If you follow those who do evil,
> Even though you do not engage in it yourself,
> Others will suspect you of evil,
> And infamy will spread.

As well as:

> Persons who keep company with base individuals will themselves
> become corrupted.

If one relies on nonvirtuous friends, all one's faults will increase and all one's qualities will degenerate. Therefore, it is said that one needs to give them up.

From the *Sutra of the Application of Mindfulness*:

> Evil friends, who are the basis for desire, anger, and ignorance, are like a poisonous tree.

Moreover, from the *Nirvana Sutra*:

> The bodhisattva's fear of bad company is not like the fear of a mad elephant. The latter will only trample the body, but the former will destroy the purity of both one's mind and one's virtue.

From *The Way of the Bodhisattva*:

> Being in the company of childish beings
> Will cause me to praise myself and belittle others.

In short, if one keeps company with unwholesome friends, their faults will rub off, and the virtuous Dharma, which has not yet arisen, will not arise. Likewise, that which has already arisen will degenerate. In such ways there are many shortcomings.

Furthermore, Lord Atisha said:

> Keep in mind that one should give up friends who arouse negative emotions and rely on friends who increase virtue.

Also, from *The Questions and Answers of the Father Teaching*:

> "Atisha, who is the worst among adversaries?"
> "Drom, the evil companion is one's archenemy."
> "Atisha, what is the most adverse circumstance for one's vows?"
> "Drom, that is women and so forth, so give them up!"

Dromtonpa himself said at one time:

> Keep skillfully away from negative friends who generate attachment and aversion.

As well as:

> If an inferior person associates with an excellent friend, then this person will become no better than a person of mediocre character.

If an excellent individual associates with a base one, then the excellent person will, without difficulty, become base.

Potowa explains the following:

If one, on top of being weak, listens to the advice of bad companions and assimilates their conduct, then one's long- and short-term aims will be mistaken.

And:

Just as remaining near dogs brings us near dog bites, if we general practitioners, and especially those ordained, stay in the proximity of young women, then in terms of this life, we will be near a bad reputation, and in terms of future lives, we will be near the lower realms.

Sharawa said:

Since women are a root of your negative emotions, don't stay in their vicinity.

Shabopa:

There is no understanding that loving but evil friends may be disastrous guides, and that angry but virtuous friends may be of benefit.

Nyugrumpa states:

You should give rise to the notion that an nonvirtuous friend is your deadly enemy. You should give rise to the notion that a bad companion is a contagious disease.

Furthermore, from the great Gyalse Togme himself:

If one relies on evil friends, unwholesomeness will increase,
Since they create obstacles to the virtuous Dharma.

And:

You who wish for happiness in all your lives,
Cast friends who are of poor character far away!

He taught this way and practiced just so.

6

RELYING ON A

SPIRITUAL FRIEND

RELYING ON the favorable circumstance of a spiritual friend:

> *When relying on the sacred spiritual friend, our faults become exhausted*
> *And our good qualities increase like the waxing moon.*
> *It is the practice of bodhisattvas to value such a sacred spiritual friend*
> *As more precious than their own body.*

When we follow or attend certain friends, our faults, such as attachment and aversion, become exhausted, and all the good qualities, such as listening, reflecting, and meditating, love, compassion, and bodhichitta, increase further and further like the waxing moon. To regard such sacred spiritual friends and excellent companions as even more precious than one's own life and body and to correctly follow them in one's thoughts and actions is the practice of bodhisattvas—their manner of following a spiritual friend.

Concerning that, from the *Sutra of the Ornamental Array*:

> Never tire of the sight of your spiritual friend. If one wonders "Why?" the answer is that, regarding spiritual friends, it is difficult to behold them and it is rare that they appear.

Moreover, this sutra teaches that there are many benefits to having been accepted by a spiritual friend, such as not falling into the lower realms, not falling into the hands of evil friends, and not easily becoming overpowered by karma and negative emotions.

More from the *Jataka Stories*:

No one should be far from the sacred ones;
With a gentle demeanor one should tend to virtue.

When we remain near them, their qualities
Will rub off on us without being deliberately rubbed in.

Furthermore, as for the need to depend on someone superior to oneself, *Purposeful Expressions* states:

Since sacredness is obtained by relying on a master,
One should rely on one who is superior to oneself.

In the Vinaya it is taught that the entirety of one's pure conduct depends on a spiritual friend.

In *Letter to a Friend* the following is said:

Through relying on a spiritual friend, pure conduct will become completely perfected.

There are two ways to rely on a spiritual friend: by means of thought and by means of deeds. Concerning the first way, there are two: training in basic faith and remembering the spiritual friend's kindness. It is taught that faith is the root and the preliminary for all pure dharmas. From a sutra:

As a preliminary engender the motherlike faith.

There are many other such statements.

As for the way of remembering the kindness, one must recall what, for instance, the *Sutra of the Ornamental Array* teaches, which is that the spiritual teacher is the one who protects one from the lower realms.

The second way of relying on a spiritual friend is through deeds. It is taught in the *Ornament of the Sutras* in the following manner:

One should attend to a spiritual teacher by means of rendering service and possessions, paying homage, and engaging in practice.

Thus, one must attend one's teacher by practicing these three ways of delighting the spiritual friend.

From *The Way of the Bodhisattva*:

One should never forsake a spiritual friend
Who is learned in the meaning of the Great Vehicle

And is supreme in the practice of the bodhisattva's path,
Even at the cost of one's life.

As well as:

Just as is described in the life story of Shri Sambhava,
Study the way of knowing how to rely on a master.

If one follows the spiritual teacher in a correct manner, all faults in one's
being will become exhausted, and all good qualities will increase. That brings
about many benefits. The opposite of all these good qualities is the fault of not
following the spiritual friend correctly.

Furthermore, Lord Atisha explained:

Dear friends, because you need a master until you reach enlightenment, follow a sacred spiritual teacher.

And:

All the qualities of the Great Vehicle, be they great or small, are
taught to arise in dependence upon a master.

When beseeched by a loud voice, "Atisha, please give us oral instructions!"
he replied, "Hey, hey! I have good ears! In order to get oral instructions, you
need faith, faith!"

Dromtonpa asked Atisha: "You who are of pure conduct, does your pure
conduct depend upon companions?"

Atisha answered: "Pure conduct certainly depends on virtuous companions!"

Dromtonpa also said:

Rely on the circumstance of a teacher day and night.
Take the sacred friend, a walking staff of virtue, as support.

Potowa elaborates:

Even though one may be weak, if one accompanies an excellent
friend, he will not allow one to be mistaken about the correct path.
He will help one to protect one's vows and engage in all that is
virtuous.

And:

In order to develop his qualities further and further, the beginner who has no understanding of the Dharma at all depends entirely on a master of the Great Vehicle. Until he attains mental stability, he must not separate from the master for even a short while. Therefore, one must persist in following a spiritual master.

Moreover, he elaborates:

If one has no respect for the masters,
No benefit will come even if one were to attend the Buddha.

Kharagpa said:

Follow a sacred master
Who is endowed with the qualities of learnedness and purity
And is free of worldly concerns.

Moreover, he said:

In a person without faith, not the slightest good qualities of any kind will appear.
Therefore, follow a spiritual master and read the sutras.

Nyugrumpa said:

Give rise to the notion of your spiritual master as being like a wish-fulfilling jewel
And of your excellent friends as being like a strong fortress.

Jayulwa said the following:

Always follow a spiritual friend, since he is the one who shows the path to liberation and omniscience.

Jayulwa himself provided an extraordinary, noble life example of correctly following his spiritual friend.

As for the need for finding inspiration in the example of sacred beings who have superior qualities to one's own, Puchungwa said:

I study all the life examples of the sacred ones; they are my inspirations.

Tazhi proclaims:

The old masters of Radreng are for me the focus of attention.

Furthermore, from Gyalse Togme himself:

> Virtue increases in dependence upon a virtuous friend.

And:

> This is the one who shows the great method for realizing the unborn.
> Attend to such a sacred being as if he were an ornament on top of
>     your head.

He taught and practiced in this manner, attending to more than forty spiritual teachers, such as the incomparable masters Sonam Dragpa and Rinpoche Sherbumpa.

7

# TAKING REFUGE

CONCERNING TAKING REFUGE, which is the gateway to the teachings:

> *Bound, themselves, in the prison of samsara,*
> *Whom are the worldly gods able to protect?*
> *Therefore, it is the practice of the bodhisattvas*
> *To go for refuge in the three unfailing Jewels.*

However grand their powers may be, great worldly gods and so forth are themselves locked in the prison of cyclic existence from which it is extremely difficult to become free. Having become helplessly bound by the tight iron fetters of suffering's origin—karma and negative emotions—how could any of them protect individuals who pursue the benefits of the higher realms and seek liberation from samsaric misery and the lower realms? They lack even the slightest capacity to provide such protection.

Therefore, when seeking protection, one takes refuge, surrendering oneself with total confidence in the precious Three Jewels, which are at all times naturally unfailing and which possess the definite ability to protect one from all the fears of existence and the temptation of peace. This is the mode of practice whereby all bodhisattvas train in the application of taking refuge.

From *The Way of the Bodhisattva*:

> Victorious One, protector of beings,
> Who endeavors to guard beings,
> Whose great fortitude dispels all fear,
> From this day forward, in you I take refuge!

What is meant by the expression "protector of beings"? The Victorious One protects all beings with a compassion free of any partiality. The expression "who endeavors to guard beings" implies that he acts for their welfare free of any partiality. "Great fortitude" means he is free from all trepidation. "Dispels all fear" means he is skilled in the methods of dispelling the fears of others.

Someone endowed with these four special features is suitable as a refuge. Since the Buddha possesses these features, but others such as Ishvara do not, the Buddha is established as the supreme refuge. Consequently, the Dharma that he taught, as well as his Sangha of followers, are also suitable refuges.

Thus, *Seventy Stanzas of Taking Refuge* states:

> The Buddha, the Dharma, and the Sangha
> Are the refuge for all those who wish for liberation.

Among the many benefits of taking refuge is that one fully enters into Buddhism.

In short, from *The Paramita Compendium*:

> If the merit of taking refuge had a form,
> Even the three-thousand-fold universe would be too small to
>  contain it.

However, if one does not feel trust from one's heart in the Three Jewels, it will be difficult for all the benefits to arise in the genuine way. The short-comings of not taking refuge are the corresponding opposites of its benefits. The important trainings, the individual ones as well as the general, must be learned elsewhere.

Furthermore, Lord Atisha said:

> Rely fully upon the objects of refuge—
> The supreme refuge, the master, and the Three Jewels.
> Rely on them with faith, the immense ground of virtue,
> Which is admiration, yearning, and certainty.

Having realized refuge-taking as the root of the Dharma, Atisha established all the monks and laypeople of Nyetang and elsewhere in the state of refuge. Thus, he became renowned as the so-called Refuge Master.

Dromtonpa also explained:

> It is difficult to be freed from the ocean of samsara;
> It is also difficult to bear all its sufferings.
> Therefore, we must seek refuge, together with all our parents.
> If you ever look for sanctuary elsewhere,
> You'll find there is none superior to the Three Jewels.

And:

> There is no teacher comparable to the Buddha;
> There is no protection comparable to the Dharma;
> There is no field comparable to the Sangha.
> Therefore, I go for refuge in them.

Potowa said:

> We should take refuge in the transcendent capable conqueror,
> Lord Buddha, who is the source of protection against our fear of
> the sufferings of samsara and the lower realms. Others, such as
> worldly gods, Ishvara, *nagas,* and sorcerers, cannot function as
> refuges, since they themselves have not transcended samsara.

He continued:

> Having thought about this again and again, our trust will further
> develop, our being will grow more pure, and the blessings will
> thereby arise. After we have taken refuge with certainty from the
> core of our hearts, we train in its precepts. Whatever we do then
> will be nothing but the activity of the Buddha. But people like us
> are not even able to think of the Buddha's wisdom as some sort of
> clever soothtelling.

Moreover:

> In the country of Yungwa, no one knew greater happiness than
> Geshe Khamlungpa, who put his trust in the Three Jewels. Also,
> in the country of Lungsho, Chen-ngawa did the same, and his
> happiness, well-being, and fame were great. It is the same with all
> others who carry out the Dharma. If we also put our trust in the
> Three Jewels, it is certain that happiness, well-being, and fame
> will occur.

Kharagpa said:

> If you rely on them, they will not deceive you.
> This is exclusively the quality of the Three Jewels,
> So always go for refuge there!

Gyalse Togme himself explains it in this way:

> Since all the worldly gods and human beings here
> Are themselves not free from their fears,
> They are powerless to protect others
> And should therefore be understood to be not the supreme,
>     permanent refuge.

> Since we seek refuge in those who are definitely able to bestow
> All temporary and ultimate happiness,
> We should be placing our trust perfectly in these Three Jewels.
> With a mind of devotion, fervently take refuge.

Moreover, he taught that while on the path, taking refuge is the supreme main part, the preliminary practice, and the way to clear obstacles. He also practiced accordingly.

# THE MAIN PART

*Demonstrating the Paths of the Three Kinds of Beings*

# THE PATH OF LESSER BEINGS

AMONG THE THREE POINTS of the main part, "Demonstrating the Paths of the Three Kinds of Beings," first is the path of the lesser beings who give up wrongdoing after having become frightened by the suffering of the lower realms.

> *All the sufferings of the lower realms, so extremely difficult to bear,*
> *Are taught by the Sage to be the fruit of one's evil actions.*
> *Therefore, it is the practice of bodhisattvas*
> *To constantly refrain from evil actions, even at the cost of one's life.*

Merely hearing of the suffering of the three lower realms induces fear, and when it actually befalls one, it is extremely difficult to bear. These sufferings of being tormented by excruciating sensations are taught by the omniscient Sage, who possesses the power to perceive the myriad karmic actions and their results as not being uncaused and not occurring from discordant causes. They are the fruition of evil actions, such as the ten nonvirtuous deeds.

Therefore, to refrain from ever undertaking evil, nonvirtuous deeds, even at the cost of one's life, is the practice whereby bodhisattvas engage in accepting good actions and rejecting evil ones.

From *Precious Garland of the Middle Way*:

> Think of what a single day is like
> In the hell realms of extreme heat or cold;
> Also remember the hungry ghosts, so emaciated due to hunger
>     and thirst;
> Look at and recall the animals whose deluded sufferings are
>     exceedingly numerous.

There are eighteen classes of hell realms, three classes of hungry ghost realms, and two classes of animal realms. It is certain that their sufferings, such as those of heat and cold, hunger and thirst, and of eating one another, are all the results of nonvirtue.

From the previous text:

> All sufferings arise from nonvirtue;
> In the same way, so do all the lower realms.

*The Way of the Bodhisattva* states the following:

> Misery, mental discomfort,
> All different kinds of fear,
> Being separated from what we desire—
> All happen because of our evil behavior.

As well as:

> How can I be definitely freed
> From nonvirtue, the cause for my suffering?
> On all occasions, day and night,
> I shall only be concerned with this.

Thus, the contemplation of karma—cause and effect—is important. As for the general reflection on the results of karma, it is the case that: (1) karmic action is certain, (2) karmic actions proliferate, (3) one will not encounter with what has not been done, and (4) that which has been done will not dissipate.

As for the specific reflection upon karma and result, there are, roughly summarized, the ten nonvirtuous ways of behaving and their opposites, the ten virtuous deeds. Each of these has its individual effects, such as the result of complete ripening, the result resembling the cause, the predominating result, and so forth. Most importantly, having pondered the way in which these effects must be experienced, each of them distinctively, we should give birth to a trusting faith in karma and its results.

If we think about the sufferings of samsara, we will give rise to renunciation and compassion. If we ponder karma and its effects, then through confident faith, we will engage in the correct way of accepting and rejecting. These are the benefits of contemplating these points. The opposite of these benefits are the faults of not contemplating.

Moreover, Lord Atisha said:

> The wise will commit absolutely no evil,
> As it results in the pain of the lower realms.

And he continues:

> Karma and its result is the only issue of real profundity. More important than beholding the face of our yidam deity is the attainment of stable confidence regarding karma, cause and effect.

Lord Atisha also set forth an example of karma and its effects:

> If the root is poisonous, the branches and leaves are also poisonous. If the root is medicinal, the branches and leaves are also medicinal. Similarly, everything done with attachment, hatred, and ignorance is nonvirtuous.

Since he taught nothing other than karma and its effect while in Western Tibet, he became renowned as the so-called Karma and Its Effect Master.

Dromtonpa also said:

> When we fall into the three lower realms, there is no happiness, only suffering.

And:

> Whatever evil and goodness we have created while alive,
> The results of both will appear some time in the future.

He continued:

> If you do not endeavor in virtuous deeds now,
> You will undoubtedly experience suffering in the future.

Also:

> Lords, don't be overconfident;
> For dependent origination is indeed subtle.

Potowa explained the following:

> If, at the present time, we were to give up the ten nonvirtuous deeds and practice the ten virtues, then even if we were to search for the three lower realms, we would not find them. If, having abandoned the ten virtuous deeds, we carelessly commit the ten nonvirtues, then even though we were to search for the higher realms and liberation, we would wander about without finding them.

Potowa continues:

> Only karma and its results are extremely profound;
> Even emptiness can be understood through logical reasoning.

Puchungwa says:

> In my old age I have now finally met with "the wise and the fool."[21]

Khamlungpa said to Puchungwa: "The spiritual friend has taught that karma and its effects alone are important, but isn't just this bit of teaching on karma and its effects difficult to teach, study, and practice?"

Puchungwa answered: "So it is."

When Langri Tangpa requested instructions from Chen-ngawa, Chen-ngawa said:

> My lord, I regard the contemplation on the effects of karma as nothing other than oral instructions.

Kharagpa said:

> The causes from which the sufferings of the lower realms appear
> Are negative actions and evil, so give them up!

Sharawa explains the following:

> Being fond of the oh-so-high teachings without studying the effects of karma is like building a castle on top of ice.

Moreover, from Gyalse Togme himself:

> All those in the lower realms are tormented by numerous sufferings,
> Such as heat and cold, hunger and thirst, and devouring one another.

He continues:

> Since all the happiness and sufferings of noble and vile beings
> Are impelled and completed by their virtue and nonvirtue,
> Do not commit evil, even at the cost of your life,
> And always endeavor in the virtuous Dharma.

Thus he taught, and practiced accordingly.

9

# THE PATH OF
# MEDIOCRE BEINGS

CONCERNING THE PATH of the mediocre beings who strive for liberation without being attached to the happiness in samsara:

> *The happiness of the three realms is like a dewdrop on the tip of*
> *a blade of grass;*
> *It perishes by itself from one instant to the next.*
> *Hence, it is the practice of a bodhisattva*
> *To strive for the supreme level of liberation, always unchanging.*

However much defiled happiness may exist in the three realms or three existences—the desire realm, the form realm, and the formless realm—all of it resembles a drop of dew on the tip of a blade of grass. Since it perishes and degenerates from moment to moment and instant by instant by itself, it is unreasonable to be attached to it.

The supreme level of liberation, free of the chains of the two obscurations, is by nature permanent, stable, unchanging, and eternal. It is perfect enlightenment. By means of the special renunciant mind inspired toward that liberation, one exerts oneself on the path of the Great Vehicle. This is the way in which all bodhisattvas train in engendering the mind that pursues complete liberation.

From *Four Hundred Verses of the Middle Way*:

> How will the one who feels no sadness in this life
> Feel devotion toward peace?

*The Way of the Bodhisattva* also states:

> Without suffering, there will be no renunciation.

Unless one perceives the entirety of existence as suffering and thus out of sadness develops a mind that longs to abandon such a state, one will not engender the dedication to strive for that liberation that pacifies all misery. One must therefore detach oneself even from the happiness of the higher realms. If one clings to it, one will not be able to transcend samsaric existence.

From a sutra:

> All those who possess a mind attached to samsara will circle forever within it.

In order to engender a renunciant mind that pursues liberation, one must understand the truth of suffering, the shortcomings of cyclic existence, and the truth of origin, the stages of samsaric engagement.

The same sutra explains the general shortcomings of samsara, which has six defects: the uncertainty of friends and enemies, the lack of satisfactory experiences, the repetition of discarding the physical body, the monotony of transmigration, the vacillation between high and low rebirth, and the loneliness of lacking companionship at the time of death. It also teaches that there are eight, three, etc. types of suffering. In terms of the specific individual sufferings, it is not only the aforementioned three lower realms that are, by nature, painful, but the three higher realms as well.

From a sutra:

> In samsara, there is not even as much happiness
> As on the tip of a needle.

Maitreya explained:

> Just as excrement lacks a sweet fragrance, the five classes of beings
> are bereft of happiness.

*Four Hundred Verses of the Middle Way* states:

> All the wise are just as frightened of the higher realms
> As they are of the hells.

At this point, it no longer suffices to focus only on the shortcomings of the lower realms, as was done in the context of those with a lesser capacity. Here, we must understand that the whole of existence is a source of suffering, resembling the interior of a burning house. Having understood it as such, we will begin to pursue liberation, and based on that, we will attain nirvana.

*Purposeful Expressions* states:

> If you realize the shortcomings in that way,
> You will quickly attain nirvana.

When one contemplates the truth of origin, the process of engaging in cyclic existence, one realizes that all the sufferings of existence are produced by the origin of karmic actions, which in return are produced by the origin of negative emotions. The root of all negative emotions is ego-clinging, and if one is able to reverse ego-clinging, one will be capable of gaining the peaceful cessation of suffering or of actualizing liberation. What does "liberation" mean in this context? It is freedom from all the bonds of karma and negative emotions.

The path that causes liberation is the practice of the three trainings. Among these three, that which actually reverses ego-clinging, the root of samsara, is the knowledge that realizes egolessness. This knowledge is based on meditative absorption. Since the root of all such qualities is discipline, at the outset discipline is very important.

From Nagarjuna's *Letter to a Friend*:

> Strive in order to reverse rebirth.

And:

> Strive for the sake of no more rebirth.

At the present time, when we have not been born into the eight unfree states but have obtained this extraordinary support of the precious human body, we must train in reversing birth. That is to say, we must persist on the path that brings about the attainment of liberation free of rebirth.

Moreover, Lord Atisha said:

> Friends, there is no happiness in this swamp of samsara. Depart for the dry land of liberation.

Atisha also taught that, although one abides purely by the three vows, if one does not engender revulsion toward cyclic existence, then this can function as the cause of samsara.

Dromtonpa says:

> Contemplate the agonies of samsara day and night. After acknowledging them, out of fear make a heartfelt wish to escape upward.

Potowa explains:

> As long as we perceive it as a palace, there is no way to attain complete liberation from wandering in samsara.

And he continues:

> Even though free from the lower realms, there is also no happiness to be found in the mere attainment of an existence as a human or a god, since the permanent stronghold has still not been captured. Therefore, one needs to understand that all of samsara is painful.

When Kyangtsa Doltsul requested oral instructions, the answer was:

> You should meditate on the shortcomings of samsara. Thereby, cyclic existence will not be something difficult to forsake, nor will liberation be something difficult to achieve.

Kharagpa explains:

> Through meditating upon the lack of happiness wherever one takes rebirth, the need to turn the mind away from all of samsara will be understood.

The text *Seventy Admonitions* also mentions:

> Samsaric beings have no happiness.

Nyugrumpa said:

> Because you wish to attain the enlightenment of the definite good, you should give rise to the notion that samsara is a prison.

Drogon explained:

> If you engender an authentic state of mind wherein you feel renunciation toward samsara, complete liberation from the three existences will occur easily and swiftly, just as when flint meets dry tinder.

Regarding the need to endeavor right now, in order to reverse cyclic existence, *Dharma through Example* states:

> In the past, I have wandered for so long in samsara. It has not come to an end by itself, and it will not do so; therefore, I need

to reverse it. Moreover, the time for reversing it is this present time when I have obtained the freedoms and riches.

In the *Blue Udder* it is taught in a similar way. Naljorpa Chenpo also explained:

Now is the time to distinguish yourself from cattle.

Neuzurpa says the following:

To turn away when face to face with the three lower realms is extremely profitable.

Furthermore, from Gyalse Togme himself:

Having understood that the nature of samsara is suffering,
Give up its cause—karma and negative emotions.
In order to obtain nirvana,
Endeavor intensely on the path to liberation.

He taught this way and practiced accordingly.

Since this path of mediocre beings is the root of the path to liberation, it is extremely important.

10

# THE PATH OF GREAT BEINGS

THERE ARE THREE POINTS that demonstrate the path of great beings, wherein liberation from the extremes of existence and peace occurs through meditating on the unity of emptiness and compassion.

1. The intention, setting one's mind upon supreme enlightenment
2. The application, cultivating the two kinds of bodhichitta
3. Training in the disciplines of the first two

> *When all our mothers, who have cherished us since beginningless time,*
>     *are suffering,*
> *Of what use then is our own happiness?*
> *Therefore, it is the practice of bodhisattvas to engender the mind of*
>     *enlightenment*
> *For the sake of liberating sentient beings beyond limit.*

Since beginningless existence, all the six classes of sentient beings, my kind old mothers, have, with intense boundless love, cherished me even more than their own lives. With immense kindness, they brought me up again and again. When each and every one of them is tormented by the usual sufferings of samsara and, in particular, by the strong and long-lasting agonies of the lower realms, what use is it if I, without giving them any thought whatsoever, pursue the happiness of the higher realms for my own benefit and, in addition, pursue liberations such as that of the arhat level of the pratyekabuddhas or the shravakas?

Pursuing my own peace and happiness without striving for a method to make all my mothers happy is extremely shameful and is an object of reproach by all the noble beings. It is the most vile deviation from the path of the Great Vehicle.

For these reasons, in order to make limitless sentient beings attain enlightenment, thereby liberating them from cyclic existence, one thinks: "Just

as all buddhas and bodhisattvas of the past engendered bodhichitta, I will also
generate the mind set upon supreme enlightenment." To arouse the mind of
enlightenment after developing loving compassion is the manner of practice
whereby all bodhisattvas generate the resolve toward great enlightenment.

Furthermore, from *Ornament of the Sutras*:

> Giving rise to the mind of enlightenment
> Means wishing for true and perfect enlightenment for the benefit
>    of others.

To apply oneself to the pursuit of that which is to be attained, perfect enlightenment for the benefit of others, is the essence of arousing the mind of
enlightenment of the Great Vehicle.

When categorizing the mind of enlightenment, *The Way of the Bodhisattva* states:

> In short, the mind of enlightenment
> Is said to have two aspects:
> The mind that aspires toward enlightenment
> And the mind that applies itself toward enlightenment.

Thus, there are the mind of enlightenment of aspiration and the mind of
enlightenment of application. As for the difference between these two, the
same text states:

> Just as one understands the difference
> Between wishing to go and actually doing so,
> In the same way should all wise ones
> Understand the progressive difference between these two.

Furthermore, the gateway to the Great Vehicle's paths of both sutra and
mantra is the mind of enlightenment. Whether or not one is counted among
the representatives of the Great Vehicle depends on whether one has or does
not have this mind.

From *The Way of the Bodhisattva*:

> If bodhichitta comes to birth in someone
> Who is suffering in the prison of samsara,
> Then in one instant, that one will be called the child of all the
>    bliss-gone ones
> And become the object of worship of gods and humans.

And:

> Today my life has born fruit;
> This human existence has been well assumed.
> I have been born into the family of the buddhas
> And become a child of the enlightened ones.

If embraced by the mind of enlightenment, merely offering a morsel of food to an animal will become an aspect of bodhisattva activity. If not embraced by it, offering even the three-thousand-fold universe filled with jewels will not, apart from being mere generosity, become an aspect of bodhisattva activity. This should also be understood as applicable to discipline and the other paramitas. This illustrates the benefits and faults of possessing or not possessing the mind of enlightenment and of embracing or not embracing one's actions with the mind of enlightenment.

In the same way, the *Sutra of the Ornamental Array*, *The Way of the Bodhisattva*, and other texts teach extensively on the benefits of the mind of enlightenment.

From the *Sutra Requested by Shridatta*:

> If the merit of the mind of enlightenment
> Had a form,
> It would fill the whole of space
> And overflow even that.

These express the benefits in summary.

What is the essence of the path of the Great Vehicle that brings about the attainment of the fruition, the two kayas? It is method and knowledge perfectly complete, the foremost methods being great compassion and bodhichitta, and the foremost knowledge being the discriminating knowledge that realizes emptiness.

*Essence of the Middle Way* states:

> Ornamented by love, compassion,
> And great knowledge,
> The seed of enlightenment is bodhichitta.
> Therefore, a learned one never abandons that.

Among the two approaches to training the mind in bodhichitta—pursuing the benefit of others and pursuing enlightenment—the former, when described according to the oral instructions of Lord Atisha, requires that one gradually trains the mind in the seven instructions, such as acknowledging sentient beings as your mothers, remembering their kindness, and so forth. When taught according to the oral instructions of the bodhisattva Shantideva, it is explained that one must train the mind through exchanging oneself with others. This will be explained below.

When the manner of mind training by means of love and compassion, which are very important in both approaches, is explained, *love* is generally described as the wish that a particular sentient being, who is deprived of happiness, be endowed with happiness. Thus, great love is wishing that all sentient beings may be endowed with happiness and the cause of happiness, which is virtue.

In the same way, *compassion* is when, focusing upon a particular sentient being who is tormented by any kind of suffering, one wishes that that being may be free from suffering. *Great compassion* is wishing that all sentient beings may be free from suffering and the cause of suffering, which is nonvirtue.

Regarding the reflection on how all sentient beings are tormented by suffering, if we first think about how we ourselves are tormented by suffering, renunciation will arise. In the same way, when we think about how others are tormented by suffering, compassion will arise.

Great compassion is the root of the path of the Great Vehicle, and in order to accomplish enlightenment, its presence is utterly essential in the beginning, middle, and end. Thinking, "May I act to endow all sentient beings with happiness and free them from suffering," one takes on the burden of benefiting others. This is superior intention, and based upon it, the authentic mind of enlightenment arises.

Concerning the latter of the two approaches, the mind training that pursues enlightenment, having perceived the necessity of great enlightenment in order to accomplish the benefit of others, we then make the wish to attain buddhahood by striving for it from the core of our hearts.

Furthermore, from Lord Atisha:

> Love and compassion are to be cultivated,
> And one should stabilize the mind of enlightenment.

He continues:

> Combined with great compassion,
> The mind of enlightenment is lauded as supreme.

On an occasion when Lord Atisha was making circumambulations in Bodhgaya, Tara and Bhrikuti magically emanated as an old woman and a young maiden, respectively. Amid their dialogue of questions and answers, they said to him, "Since you wish to become enlightened quickly, train in love, compassion, and the mind of enlightenment!"

Through this, he gave birth to certainty. Many such events are described in his life story.

The yogi Chagtri Chog was thirty years old when he met Lord Atisha and asked him for oral instructions. Lord Atisha replied:

> From this day forward, do not keep your name in mind, do not keep your family in mind, and do not keep your country in mind. Cultivate nothing but love and compassion, the mind of enlightenment.

Because he did just that, it is said that he attained the supreme accomplishment at the age of thirty-five.

Dromtonpa also said:

> Cultivate love and compassion abundantly and make the mind of enlightenment firm.

He continued:

> Love, compassion, and the mind of enlightenment are the causes that establish the two great benefits for oneself and others.

Once Dromtonpa told Naljorpa Chenpo:

> Although you may possess a meditation that is not destroyed even by the beating of a large drum close to your ear, if you lack love, compassion, and the mind of enlightenment, there will come a time when you must do confessions day and night.

Geshe Gonpawa explained:

> The root of omniscient wisdom depends on the two accumulations, the root of the two accumulations depends on the mind of enlightenment, and the root of the mind of enlightenment depends on love and compassion.

In Potowa's *Dharma through Example*:

> No matter what activities you may engage in with your three doors, carry all of them out as you train in love, compassion, and the mind of enlightenment.

Regarding demonstrating love through an example, an old woman petitioned Potowa: "What does Atisha's 'meditation on love' mean?" Potowa answered: "Just as you love and hold very dearly your son, called Tole, you should consider everyone else with exactly the same affection." The old woman exclaimed: "Mercy! Even if I were to meditate a hundred days, that would not happen." Potowa then said that she had understood the point.

I believe this primarily demonstrates affectionate loving-kindness.

In the context of compassion, Dromtonpa told a person from Kham named Jampal whose legs were injured: "Now, if your old mother were in front of you being bitten by a ferocious dog, and there was no one else around, you would certainly stagger toward her without remembering your injured legs. In the same way, if one gives rise to an unfabricated mind that perceives sentient beings as one's mothers, overwhelming compassion will come about the moment one sees the suffering of a sentient being."

In the context of giving rise to the mind of enlightenment, one named Shangmon Khidrug asked: "Atisha's 'bringing forth the mind of enlightenment,' what is that about?" Potowa answered: "It refers to establishing all sentient beings in the state of buddhahood after having liberated them from suffering in samsara." The man replied: "Oh dear! That seems to require such great courage!"

Potowa furthermore told:

> After we have given rise to a mind set on supreme enlightenment, we should develop the courage to act for the welfare of sentient beings.

Langri Tangpa also stated:

> Actually, everything depends on courage.

Shabopa explained:

> In order for omniscience to take root, one should train one's being in the mind of enlightenment.

Jayulwa said:

> Since it is the life-tree of the path to omniscience and liberation, train in the mind of enlightenment.

Rinchen Gangpa explained the following:

Lacking the inclination to benefit others,
The resolutions of the bodhichittas of aspiration and application do
    not arise,
Nor will one master the Mahayana teachings.
Therefore, compassion and love are so very important.

Furthermore, from Gyalse Togme himself:

Having cast far away one's own happiness,
One must take up the burden of suffering for the benefit of all.
But if one casts far away one's regard for the host of sentient beings,
What use is it to obtain the holy Dharma of the Great Vehicle?

Therefore, the one who, in order to liberate limitless sentient beings,
Engenders the mind set upon supreme unsurpassable enlightenment,
Who gives up self-interest and carries out, directly and indirectly, the
    benefit of others,
That one is a sublime being.

As the core of his spiritual practice, he himself is engaged in cultivating love, compassion, and the mind of enlightenment.

11

# CULTIVATING THE EXCHANGE
# OF ONESELF FOR OTHERS

As FOR APPLICATION—the cultivation of the two kinds of bodhichitta—first there is the cultivation of relative bodhichitta, and next there is the cultivation of absolute bodhichitta. Concerning the first topic, there are two aspects:

1. Cultivating the exchange of oneself for others during meditative equipoise
2. Bringing negative circumstances onto the path during post-meditation

> *All suffering, without exception, springs from the desire for*
>    *one's own happiness;*
> *Perfect enlightenment is born from a mind intent on benefiting others.*
> *Therefore, it is the practice of bodhisattvas*
> *To authentically exchange one's own happiness for the sufferings of others.*

Here in this place of cyclic existence, however many grave and trivial sufferings there may be, all of them spring, without exception, from holding oneself dear, from desiring one's own happiness. Whatever mundane or supramundane happiness and benefits there may be, such as the ultimate happiness at the level of perfect enlightenment, all spring, or are born, from a mind that wishes to benefit others, that holds others dear.

Therefore, regarding others as more dear than oneself, one gives away whatever happiness and virtue one may possess to sentient beings, while having complete disregard for oneself. By means of taking upon oneself all the suffering and evil that may be in the mindstreams of other sentient beings, one exchanges happiness and suffering. In other words, one authentically reverses the two attitudes of clinging to self-cherishing and casting others far away. This is the mode of practice whereby all bodhisattvas cultivate exchanging oneself for others.

*The Way of the Bodhisattva* states:

> Whoever wishes to quickly protect
> Himself and all others,
> Should engage in the sacred secret
> Called "exchanging oneself for others."

Based on the wish to protect self and others from the fears of existence and the temptation of peace, it is taught that one must exchange oneself for others. Concerning the faults of clinging to self-cherishing and the qualities of holding others dear, the same scripture reads:

> However much happiness exists in this world,
> All of it springs from wishing for the happiness of others;
> However much suffering exists in this world,
> All of it springs from desiring one's own happiness.

> What need is there for lengthy explanations!
> The childish work for their own benefit,
> The sages act for the welfare of others.
> Consider the difference between these two!

As for the faults of not exchanging oneself for others, the same scripture states:

> If one does not authentically exchange
> One's own joy for others' misery,
> Enlightenment will not be accomplished,
> Nor will there be any happiness in samsara.

The benefits of exchanging oneself for others are also implicitly demonstrated, and the same scripture teaches many lines of reasoning as to how one, for instance, avoids pitfalls in the practice of exchanging oneself for others.

Exchanging oneself for others means mainly that, by interchanging the two attitudes—cherishing the self and rejecting others—a frame of mind is brought forth that cherishes others as dearly as oneself and that completely disregards the self as though it were other.

Concerning this, from *Precious Garland of the Middle Way*:

> May all their evil ripen upon myself,
> And may all my virtue, without exception, ripen upon them.

*The Way of the Bodhisattva* states also:

> I should give myself to others
> And apprehend others as myself.

Moreover, from *Mind Training*:

> "I," the root of evil karma,
> Is a thing to be thrown far away.
> "Other," the source of enlightenment,
> Is a thing to be embraced tightly.

Lord Atisha said:

> When the faults of confusion, attachment, and aversion are about
>     to arise,
> Train in the mind that exchanges oneself for others.

And he continues:

> Give all the happiness there is to others;
> Take all the suffering there is upon yourself.
> Give profit and victory to others;
> Take loss and defeat upon yourself.

Chen-ngawa said:

> All worldly beings hold themselves more dear than others, but we
> need to regard others as more dear than ourselves.

As justification, he taught extensively about the faults of clinging to self-cherishing and the qualities of holding others dear.

Langri Tangpa said:

> In short, whether in actuality or in thought,
> I offer all prosperity and happiness to all my mothers
> And shall secretly take upon myself
> All their suffering and afflictions.

He explained further:

> No matter how many profound teachings I have opened up and
> looked into, all faults indeed turn out to be my own, and all good
> qualities those of the noble sentient beings. The key point of that

is to give all gain and victory to others and to take loss and defeat upon myself. Besides this, there is nothing more to understand.

Moreover:

> Shabopa and I have eighteen "human" methods and one "horse" method—altogether nineteen.[22]

> The human methods imply that after having engendered a mind set upon supreme enlightenment, one directs every undertaking toward the welfare of sentient beings.

> Now as for the horse method: Holding on to self-cherishing does not allow the mind of enlightenment that has not yet arisen to arise or where it has arisen to remain and increase further. Therefore, one turns away from self-cherishing and trains in harming it as much as possible while wholeheartedly benefiting sentient beings as much as one can.

Shabopa once said:

> Until we perceive ourselves as the enemy, even a master, etc....will not be able to benefit us. If we see ourselves as the enemy, then everyone will bring benefit.

And:

> During the span of this short life, please endeavor to tame this demon as much as you can.

More:

> Having seen ego-clinging as the enemy, this profound teaching of abandoning this demon is called "the teaching that dispels the evil spirit."

Geshe Namo proclaimed:

> As soon as you cut the torma, it is cutting the head of ego-clinging!

Chekawa said:

> Drive all blame into a single direction
> And train in perceiving the kindness of everybody.

And:

> Train in alternating "giving and receiving";[23]
> Let them ride on your breath.

The detailed method of practice should be known from teachings such as those of the Great Hearing Lineage.

Furthermore, from Gyalse Togme himself:

> Since it is the root of benefiting others, meditate on exchanging yourself for others.

And he continues:

> After you have understood ego-clinging as the enemy, give up conquering other adversaries.
> After you have understood the qualities of sentient beings, carry all beings on the top of your head.

And:

> With the power of great love, one wishes
> That all the sufferings of others ripen upon oneself,
> And that all one's happiness and virtue ripen upon others.
> Such an unfabricated one-pointed state of mind
> Is the supreme mind of enlightenment, exchanging oneself
>     with others.

He himself made this the core of his practice.

12

# BRINGING LOSS
# ONTO THE PATH

*If someone, swayed by great desire,*
*Steals all one's wealth or incites others to do so,*
*It is the practice of bodhisattvas to dedicate to that person*
*One's physical body, enjoyments, and virtues of the three times.*

If any sentient being, overpowered by desirous craving, directly steals all our enjoyments and wealth or else incites another to engage in such theft, not only should we refrain from becoming furious with that individual and trying to return harm for harm, we should instead, with even greater benevolence, further dedicate and offer the harm-doer our physical body, which we cherish so dearly, and whatever enjoyments and virtues of the three times we may possess. Such is the manner of practice of all bodhisattvas whereby loss is brought onto the path.

From *The Way of the Bodhisattva*:

> While all my property I'll leave behind,
> Evil deeds will always accompany me.

And:

> Because I strive for liberation,
> I should not fetter myself with possessions and honor.
> Therefore why should I be angry with those
> Whose pursuit is to free me from my fetters?

Since wealth and honor are the sources of numerous faults, it is unreasonable that one should be happy when they are acquired. The one who creates hindrances to our wealth and glory and the one who steals our riches and so forth is the one who naturally frees us from these mental fetters and acts as a door-bolt that deters us from the lower realms. Therefore, we should acknowledge their kindness by further providing them with our body, enjoyments, roots of virtue, and so forth. It is senseless to become angry and dislike them.

Furthermore, from *The Way of the Bodhisattva*:

> In my past, I inflicted the same harm on others.

Considering that the obstacles made to my honor and gain and the theft of my enjoyments by others in this life are retribution for myself having inflicted similar harms on others during past lives, I should refrain from hostility. What follows in this text, in terms of the inflicting of suffering and so forth, is to be understood in the same way.

Moreover, from Lord Atisha:

> Do not be angry at the one who causes harm.
> If you are irritated at the harm-doer, how are you going to meditate on
>     patience?

He continues:

> Wealth and honor are to be given up;
> Arrogant pride should always be discarded.

And:

> Since wealth and honor are the lassos of demons, throw them
> away like pebbles on the path.

Kharagpa explained:

> Wealth and honor are ropes that fetter
> And obstacles to merit and virtuous practice.

Potowa said:

> If we do not cling to anything as our own, we will be free from
> enemies and need not accumulate hatred. When faced with mi-
> nor hardships, patience will automatically occur. As the saying
> goes, "When riches are absent, thieves will not approach. When
> goods are absent, bandits will not arrive." When an enemy ap-
> proaches your wealth and so on, it is your own reaping. Therefore,
> it is unreasonable to feel hostile toward others.

Geshe Chen-ngawa explained:

> For example, unless you have set up a target, there is nothing for
> the arrow to hit. That the arrow hits is the result of having set up
> the target. When we have set up the target of our own past nega-
> tive actions, we will be hit by the arrows of harm from others in
> this life. It is therefore inappropriate to feel rage toward others.

The same can be applied to the causes of suffering and so forth described
hereafter.

Moreover, from Gyalse Togme himself:

> After those attached to wealth or hateful toward me
> Have stolen all my possessions,
> If it is even only for one day that I happen to be without nourishing
>     food and drink,
> At that time, I should remember my promise.

He taught that we must remember our promise to foster benefit as repay-
ment for harm. The next chapters also relate to this. He continues:

> If someone carries off all my enjoyments,
> I will dedicate, from the core of my heart, thinking,
> "May those enjoyments, my physical body, and other pleasures,
> As well as all my virtue without exception, become the cause for his
>     well-being."

Thus, he made prayers and dedication, and practiced accordingly.

13

# BRINGING SUFFERING
# ONTO THE PATH

*Even if someone were to cut off one's head,*
*Though one is free from the slightest fault,*
*It is the practice of bodhisattvas to take all wrongdoing upon oneself*
*Through the force of compassion.*

It might be that while I have not done the slightest wrong, such as having inflicted harm elsewhere, others, whoever they may be, nevertheless sever all my bodily limbs and also try to cut off my most noble feature, my head. I shall then refrain from fury and retaliation in the form of violence or an attempt to slay them. In addition, I know that they will experience suffering in the future because of having committed such a heavy evil action. By the power of compassion that wishes these evildoers to be free from evil and suffering, I will therefore take upon myself the unwholesome causes within their mindstreams and all resultant suffering. Such is the manner of practice whereby all bodhisattvas bring suffering onto the path.

From *The Way of the Bodhisattva*:

> The causes for happiness appear rarely,
> While the causes for suffering are extremely numerous.

At the time of patience, whereby we joyfully accept suffering, we should neither yearn for happiness nor become discouraged by suffering. This explains how to equalize happiness and suffering. Furthermore, in the context of "the patience that does not take offense at harm-doers," it is said:

> If, when you are overpowered by negative emotions,
> You could kill even your most cherished self,

> How will you then ever refrain
> From harming the bodies of others?
>
> Toward those who now are governed by negative emotions
> And therefore try to kill you and so on,
> You may not feel vast compassion;
> But to become aggressive, how terrible!

Since negative emotions make people so crazy that they will even kill themselves, it is not surprising that they harm others. Therefore, since also the person who kills oneself is, moreover, possessed by the evil spirit of negative emotions, it is appropriate to cultivate compassion, thinking, "How pitiful!" but it is unreasonable to become angry.

More from *The Way of the Bodhisattva*:

> Both the weapon and my body
> Are the cause for my suffering.
> They pulled out their weapons, while I held out my body.
> At whom then should I be angry?

In such ways it is taught that when harm befalls one's own body, one needs to remember that this is also the fault of clinging to the body as one's own. In *Mind Training* it is taught that the occurrence of harm to one's body is the wheel of sharp weapons of one's past evil karma, with which one has previously caused harm to others.

Lord Atisha also said:

> When your body is harmed,
> Consider it to be your past karma.

Dromtonpa also explained:

> Even though your body has been cut into a thousand pieces,
> Never become distressed!
> Now don the armor of patience!

Chen-ngawa told the following:

> All worldly beings regard happiness as more precious than suf-
> fering. But for us it is the opposite—we must regard suffering as
> more dear than happiness.

To explain this, he taught extensively about the faults of attachment in defiling happiness and about the benefits of joyfully accepting suffering.

Concerning the cultivation of patience through compassion and love, he explained:

> When, for example, a lunatic causes harm to others, all those who know him and have lived before in the same area will not rebuke him. They will say, "Oh how pitiful, how sad!" and will not retaliate. In the same way, the one who harms you is a tremendous lunatic possessed by the demon of fierce negative emotions. Therefore, you should cultivate loving-kindness, thinking, "How sad!" and not become angry.

Kharagpa proclaimed:

> Since all our present happiness and suffering
> Depends upon our past actions,
> You have no choice
> But to take as help whatever arises.

Shabopa also said:

> We fail to understand that these miseries and injuries are circumstances conducive to the Dharma.

Moreover, Gyalse Togme himself stated the following:

> After someone, having become overpowered by anger and pride,
> Delivers great wounds to my body
> And the time comes for me to surely die,
> At that time, may I remember my promise.

He continues:

> All those who cut off my limbs,
> May I cut off their suffering and negative emotions.

This promise of benefit in return for harm is taught as being one among the four liberations of Shakya Shri and as one among the twelve practices of the Dharma Lord Gotsang. The bodhisattva himself practiced accordingly. For example, his exalted life story describes how he took over the fleas that were tormenting someone else.

14

# BRINGING DISGRACE
# ONTO THE PATH

*Even if someone proclaims all kinds of defamation about me*
*Throughout the three-thousand-fold universe,*
*It is the practice of bodhisattvas*
*To praise that person's qualities repeatedly with a loving attitude.*

Even if someone broadcasts all kinds of defamation about us surreptitiously, proclaiming our faults, so that such ill repute comes to pervade the three-thousand-fold universe, we will not only refrain from returning the harm. Instead of furiously uttering insults at him, we will, with a loving attitude that wishes the harm-doer mental joy, happiness, and well-being, furthermore declare this person's good qualities to everyone. Such is the manner of practice whereby all bodhisattvas bring disgrace onto the path.

From *Precious Garland of the Middle Way*:

One who is himself uncivil will hear unpleasantries.

An incident of disparagement toward us is said to be the result of having uttered harsh words in the past. Similarly, it is also explained that when the sharp weapons of our own negative karmic actions, for instance, casting aspersions upon others, return to us, it is unsuitable to become angry toward others.

Not only that, *The Way of the Bodhisattva* says the following:

"Because they harm themselves"
We are angry when they slander us.
But how is it that you do not begrudge those
Who slander others beside yourself?

Thus, even when examining the so-called disgrace, one discovers that there is no reason for anger and that it is illogical to become hostile.

Moreover, from *The Way of the Bodhisattva*:

> The honors of praise and fame
> Will bring you neither merit nor long life.

In this way, fame and so forth are utterly devoid of any essence to which one should be attached. Also:

> For the sake of fame
> One is even willing to give up wealth or to be killed.
> Yet, what can mere words of honor do when one is dead?
> And whom can they delight?

Since it is taught that attachment toward fame produces faults, it is inappropriate to relish it.

Moreover, Lord Atisha explained:

> When you hear unpleasant words,
> Regard them as an echo.

A student said to the yogi Sherab Dorje: "There are some people who speak quite badly of us." The yogi answered: "Humans speak about humans, what else? Cut through your divisive talk immediately."

To Shenton it was told:

> If you have been saying, "He said such and such…," then since there is even gossip about those of very high position, you should confess to having engaged in slander.

Sharawa said:

> No matter how much one would praise Khamlungpa, Neuzurpa, and Drapa, it was for them no different from talking about earth and rocks, and so they remained at ease. In the future everyone will have very sensitive ears and will therefore experience hardship.

As it is said in their life stories, even though Geshe Langri Tangpa, Neuzurpa, and others directly encountered defamation and slander, they did not become angry but practiced patience.

As to the inappropriateness of feeling attachment toward fame and so forth, Lord Atisha said:

> Since all words of praise and fame are deceptive seductions, expel them just like spit.

Kharagpa proclaimed:

> Fame is the deceptive flatter of the demons.

Nyugrumpa said:

> You should give rise to the notion of regarding fame and glory as an echo.

Furthermore, from Gyalse Togme himself:

> Since fame and glory are pointless, give up clinging to them.

And:

> An unbearable tale of ill repute might resound throughout the ten
>     directions
> So that as they hear it, all sentient beings will feel disgusted with me.
> If I see, hear, or recollect such,
> At that time, may I remember my promise.

In this way, not only did he not feel angry even if others circulated tales of ill repute about him, but with a loving mind he prayed that their good qualities would resound throughout the ten directions. Aside from expressing others' good qualities, it was impossible for this great bodhisattva to declare the faults of others. By this link of dependency, all masters and everyone else contemporary with the bodhisattva offered him nothing but admiration, praise, and veneration, as is frequently told in his life story.

15

# BRINGING SLANDER
# ONTO THE PATH

*Even if someone, amid a crowd of many people,*
*Reveals one's faults and utters harsh words,*
*It is the practice of the bodhisattvas to bow to that one respectfully*
*With the notion that this is one's spiritual teacher.*

If someone, in the midst of a great and vast gathering of beings, announces, "From a spiritual perspective, you have such and such fault, from a mundane standpoint you have this and that flaw…," and then voices a variety of harsh and extremely negative statements that heap abuse upon us and directly reveal our hidden failings, we will refrain from returning the harm by becoming angry and exposing that person's secret shortcomings in retaliation. Instead we will, in addition, bow respectfully to that person with the notion that this is our exceedingly kind spiritual teacher. Such is the manner of practice whereby all bodhisattvas bring slander onto the path.

From *The Way of the Bodhisattva*:

> When there are others who despise me,
> Why do I become happy when someone praises me?
> If there are others who praise me,
> Why do I then become unhappy when someone despises me?

It is taught that it is senseless to feel delighted when praised and upset when defamed. More from *The Way of the Bodhisattva*:

> If he is not there, it does not occur;
> If he is present, it comes to be.
> Since this enemy is the cause for patience,
> How can I say that he prevents it?

Moreover:

> Because of those with such aggressive states of mind,
> My patience does arise.
> They are indeed the cause for patience
> And are therefore worthy of honor, in the same way as the sacred
>     Dharma.

Someone may, with an aggressive state of mind, create situations extremely difficult to tolerate by revealing our hidden faults, heaping abuse upon us, and so on. We should then recognize this to be the spiritual master and the supreme oral instructions and should respectfully repay the kindness of that person. Anger, it is taught, would be inadmissible.

Likewise, *The Way of the Bodhisattva* states:

> Praise and so forth make one distracted
> And also destroy renunciation.

This shows the faults of being attached to praise and so forth.

Moreover:

> Therefore, those who remain near me
> To destroy my praise and the like
> Are truly there protecting me
> From falling into lower realms.

This shows how those who create an obstacle to one being praised bring an end to the lower realms.

Moreover, from Lord Atisha:

> The supreme spiritual teacher is the one who attacks your hidden
> flaws; the supreme oral instruction is that which lands directly
> upon your hidden faults. Enemies, obstacles, sickness, and suf-
> fering—those are supreme inspirations.

Shabopa said:

> I will do nothing but reveal your hidden faults.
> If you will then refrain from getting angry, stay here.
> But if not, leave!

He said this to all disciples who arrived before him.

From Potowa:

> Since we ourselves invited those who declare our imperfections and
> failings and completely expose our hidden flaws, we ought not to
> be hateful but instead repay their kindness.

Chen-ngawa explained:

> As for cultivating patience in the manner of master and disciple,
> if there is no enemy to inflict harm, there will be no patience.
> Therefore, when others abuse us and so forth, they should be rec-
> ognized as the master who bestows tolerance. Without becoming
> angry, cultivate this with delight and a feeling of gratitude for their
> kindness. Thus, think of yourself as the student who absorbs
> patience.

Langri Tangpa spoke as follows:

> When, out of jealousy, others
> Abuse and attack me in unjust ways,
> I should take such unwarranted losses upon myself
> And offer the victory to others.

Furthermore, from Gyalse Togme himself:

> When someone with the eye of aggression amid many beings
> Humiliates me with terrible statements difficult to bear,
> So that I have no chance even to lift my head upright,
> May I, at that time, remember my promise.

He continues:

> Even if I see an enraged person frowning with intense wrath,
> Who, before the eyes of a crowd of many people,
> Personally slanders me with assorted vile remarks
> That strike at my secret shortcomings,
>
> May I then, wishing to benefit him, since this affectionate one
> Cuts through the poisonous tree of my pride,
> Cut down his own venomous tree of suffering
> With the sharp weapon of skillful intelligence and great love.

He taught this and practiced accordingly. These principles are virtuous practices whereby we can refrain from retaliating against those who have disgraced

us, slandered us, caused us suffering, and so forth. They should be practiced in all contexts of the lesser as well as the greater vehicles. In particular, according to the Great Vehicle, one must provide for harm-doers, wishing to establish them in perfect enlightenment. A sutra says:

> Those who abuse me and make me unhappy…may they all become enlightened.

*The Way of the Bodhisattva* states:

> May those scorning me
> Or causing me any other harm,
> Those who are humiliating me and insulting me,
> All have the fortune to fully awaken.

This is how the eight worldly pursuits are equalized from a relative perspective. As for their sameness from an ultimate standpoint, *The Way of the Bodhisattva* states:

> Therefore, among all these empty things,
> What is there to gain and what is there to lose?

All finding, gaining, losing, and so forth are taught to be equal from the perspective of the ultimate.

16

BRINGING INGRATITUDE

ONTO THE PATH

*Even if someone for whom I have cared for as dearly as my own child*
*Perceives me as an enemy,*
*It is the practice of bodhisattvas to love this one devotedly,*
*Just as a mother loves her child stricken by disease.*

Even if a person whom I have unceasingly nurtured with material goods
and Dharma as dearly as though he were my own son views me as his enemy
and inflicts harm upon me in every possible way with his body, speech, and
mind, I will, nevertheless, refrain from animosity and in no way maliciously
return the harm.

An old mother does not just refrain from returning the harm that her sick
or possessed son may inflict on her in various ways; in addition, she is very
loving toward him, wishing that he may be free from evil spells or sickness.
In the same way, the one who causes harm has fallen under the power of negative emotions and therefore shows such great ingratitude toward me. To cultivate exceedingly great love for this one, wishing that he must by any means
become free from all negative emotions, is the practice whereby all bodhisattvas bring the ingratitude of others onto the path. Or one could say, this is
like the love of a mother who eagerly wishes that her son, who is afflicted by
disease, may swiftly recover.

*Ornament of the Sutras* states the following:

> The wise will disregard shortcomings
> In people who are always at fault and behave without self-control,
> Saying instead, "While not wanting to, they have become ungrateful."
> Therefore, they fully increase their compassion toward those beings.

Even though childish beings who are without free will due to the power of
negative emotions show their ingratitude, the wise bodhisattvas will not see
any fault in them but, it is taught, will increase their compassion toward such
people.

In *Four Hundred Verses of the Middle Way* it is said:

> Like a mother who is especially affectionate
> Toward her ailing son,
> All bodhisattvas are in the same way especially loving
> Toward those who are unkind.

*The Way of the Bodhisattva* likewise states:

> Although they are not wished for,
> These sicknesses arise.
> And likewise, although they are not wished for,
> Negative emotions persistently arise.

More:

> Don't feel saddened by all the desires
> Of childish people, always in conflict with one another.
> "Their mental states are produced by negative emotions."
> Thus, we should think, and treat them lovingly.

Having observed that it is the nature of all immature beings who have fallen
under the sway of negative emotions to angrily inflict harm upon their bene-
factors, we should act with even more affectionate love toward them.

Furthermore, Lord Atisha said:

> When encountering a particular object requiring patience, don't re-
> act impatiently, and don't say, "This is too difficult."

In *Mind Training* it is said:

> When, presently, evil is returned for the good we have done for
> someone, this is taught as the returning of the sharp weapon of
> negative karma that we once created by showing ingratitude in re-
> turn for kindness.

Dromtonpa explained:

> Never dispose of a sense of shamefulness and embarrassment.
> Even though you may benefit others, they may harm you in return.

Even though you may teach, in response they may accumulate
evil. There are so many beings who answer good with bad.

Thus he said, and Puchungwa too has taught in the same way. Langri
Tangpa said:

Even if the one whom I have helped
And in whom I have great hopes
Instead irrationally causes harm,
May I regard this one as my spiritual guide.

Furthermore, ungrateful people are naturally of bad character and accumulate intense evil. Perceiving all those ungrateful people, who are oppressed
with great suffering, as rare objects of love, one should come to regard them
as precious.

And:

When seeing sentient beings of bad character
Who are oppressed by fierce evil and suffering,
May I cherish them, for this is as rare
As the discovery of a treasury of jewels.

Chekawa said:

Though damage may be done in return for help,
Cultivate great compassion in return for even that.
The sublime beings of this world
Respond with goodness even toward the return of evil.

Also:

Always meditate on the most volatile situation.

Focus especially on that which presents difficulties for mind training—
people who cause harm in return for your benefit, hateful enemies, obstacle
makers, and competitors, and then cultivate a special loving-kindness for those.

Moreover, Gyalse Togme himself said:

The ones who cause harm to myself and to my interests,
Or do harm to the teachings and to all beings,
When I remember, hear, or see these wrongful people,
I understand them to be superior objects of compassion.

Hence, through praising and honoring them and speaking pleasing
   words,
I must benefit them directly where I can,
And where I can't, it is important that I, with fierce love and
   compassion,
Dedicate to them all virtue and happiness, however much I possess.

People we had great hopes in may deceive us and may inflict harm in return for our help. If we do not give rise to compassion and altruism toward
them, our mind is not trained. Therefore, we must especially meditate upon
those.

Accordingly, Gyalse Togme made this his main practice.

17

# BRINGING DEFAMATION
# ONTO THE PATH

*Even if a person equal to or inferior to myself*
*Defames me due to the force of pride,*
*It is the practice of the bodhisattvas to venerate this one*
*Like the master upon the crown of my head.*

If some person either equal to me in status, appearance, wealth, and qualities or else inferior to me has become swayed by pride and so despises and defames me in various ways, I will refrain from becoming angry. Not only will I do so but on top of that I will bow down to him respectfully with my body, speech, and mind. As though he were my kind guru, I will carry him above the crown of my head. Such is the manner of practice whereby bodhisattvas bring defamation onto the path.

From *The Way of the Bodhisattva*:

Even if beings cause me much harm,
I shall strive to bring them only goodness.

And:

Although many beings may trample and stamp upon my head,
Even at the risk of dying may I delight the protectors of the world.

And:

Likewise, may we not belittle
Even the most feeble harm-doer.

Whoever causes harm, high ones or low ones, after one has seen them to be like buddhas, one should pay them respect.

It is inappropriate to disregard a harm-doer, even though he may be feeble. If you return harm for the harm inflicted upon you, you and the harm-doer will become flawed, for the opponent's hatred will further increase and you will fall away from your virtuous trainings. If you do not cause harm in return, from then on you will become faultless, a being who is endowed with patience.

It is thus taught in the same scripture. In particular, patience toward those who are weak and cause great harm is, among all kinds of patience, one of great wonder.

*Ornament of the Sutras* also mentions patience for those who are weak. Generally, one should regard sentient beings as similar to gurus and wish-fulfilling jewels.

Nagarjuna explained:

> All phenomena conducive to enlightenment,
> Their cause is all sentient beings.
> Therefore, all those who wish for perfect enlightenment
> Regard all sentient beings as the guru.

From the *Compendium of Trainings*:

> They are like a wish-fulfilling jewel,
> An excellent vase, a wish-fulfilling cow,
> The guru, and the deity;
> Thus, I should pay respect to them.

*The Way of the Bodhisattva* states that we should respect sentient beings just as we do the buddhas.

Furthermore, Lord Atisha has said:

> Since the ego is the root of negative karma, let go and toss it away like the corpse of your dead father. Since others are the source of enlightenment, hold them tightly as if you had discovered a precious wish-fulfilling jewel.

Chen-ngawa also said:

> Worldly beings hold the Buddha as more dear than sentient beings, but for us it is the opposite—we must regard all sentient beings as more dear than the Buddha.

When explaining this, he taught extensively how thereby not the least bit of disrespect will occur toward the Buddha and how one needs to cherish all sentient beings through the four causes, such as knowing them to be our parents and so forth.

Langri Tangpa said:

> I shall hold dear all sentient beings
>   And consider them as precious,
>   Thinking that they accomplish a purpose
>   Even greater than that of a wish-fulfilling jewel.

Sharawa said the following:

> We must not give up loving-kindness toward sentient beings and must respect all sentient beings as no different from the Buddha.

He continues:

> The one who makes trouble is the one who purifies our wrongdoing of having inflicted harm on others in the past. He is the seed for developing patience. Therefore, it is taught that we must acknowledge the exceedingly great kindness of such persons and not forsake them. If with regard to any type of harm-doer we happen to think, "I shall return harm with harm and never help," and we allow the span of a practice session to elapse without applying an antidote, it is taught that we have forsaken sentient beings.

Furthermore, from Gyalse Togme himself:

> Whether or not I am at fault,
>   When anyone high, low, or equal to me
>   Harms me in any way,
>   At that time may I remember my promise.

He continues:

> Since the one who causes trouble is your master, place him respectfully on the crown of your head.

If one has a benevolent intention toward a harm-doer, then the disciplines of mind training and most samayas are included within that. He taught this and, accordingly, also made it his chief practice.

18

# BRINGING DECLINE
# ONTO THE PATH

*Even if I am deprived of a livelihood, constantly belittled by everyone,*
*And stricken by a severe illness or demonic influence,*
*It is the practice of bodhisattvas to take upon oneself*
*All the suffering and evil of all beings without becoming depressed.*

We may either have lacked wealth and enjoyments from the very beginning, or it may be that we were previously in possession of them but that since
then they have been plundered by enemies or become exhausted. The ability
to acquire even just food and clothes, which serve the purpose of sustaining our
lives, may also have been lost, and we may have thus become destitute. Not only
that, but people may be constantly making us an object of scorn and contempt.
And on top of that, having been stricken by a severe illness, such as leprosy,
and also attacked by a vicious demonic influence, such as an evil spirit, we may
have become completely miserable.

Yet judging from the torments of one's own suffering, we must still think
how unbearable must be the suffering of others and thereby with the strength
of compassion take upon ourselves all the suffering and evil of all sentient beings. To carry this out with fortitude, free from faintheartedness and the timid-
ity of thinking, "How will I ever endure such decline and loss?" is the manner
of practice whereby all bodhisattvas bring decline onto the path.

From *The Way of the Bodhisattva*:

Without suffering, there is no renunciation.

And:

Furthermore, concerning the qualities of suffering,
Through sadness, haughtiness is cleared away.

This addresses the way of reflecting upon the qualities of suffering.
Moreover:

> When fishermen, farmers, and butchers,
> Thinking merely of their own survival,
> Tolerate the miseries of heat and cold,
> How can I then not bear the same to bring about the happiness of
> beings?

And:

> For the sake of satisfying my desires,
> I have undergone a thousand times
> The torments of being burned in hell,
> Thereby achieving nothing for myself and others.

This shows that it is reasonable to bear with the hardships of suffering
when accomplishing that which is truly meaningful. Moreover:

> Therefore, disregard harm
> And be able to withstand suffering.

And:

> If, when feeling discouraged, one discards effort,
> How then will there ever be liberation from misery?

Through these examples and others, it is often taught how one brings any
occurrence of suffering and what is undesirable onto the path through developing fortitude free from depression.

From *Precious Garland of the Middle Way*:

> Even if you have degenerated to be like a hungry ghost,
> Do not become discouraged.

Moreover, Lord Atisha said:

> When you have become depressed,
> You should uplift your mind.

Potowa explained:

> Some traders say that when it snows, it is good for the horse's hooves, and when it rains in the evening, enemies will not approach. In the same way, sicknesses, poverty, and abuse, including even the suffering experienced in a dream, have numerous qualities, such as the purification of evil and so forth, when being brought onto the path.

Kharagpa spoke the following:

> Even the slightest suffering now
> Exhausts the evil you have done in the past;
> In the future, you will certainly be happy.
> So cultivate a liking for suffering.
>
> Adverse circumstances are the spiritual adviser;
> Obstacles are admonishments to virtuous practice;
> Suffering is the broom that sweeps away evil;
> Do not look upon these as unpleasant misfortunes.

And Chekawa has said:

> Rely continuously on a happy mind alone.

And:

> When you suffer, carry along everyone's suffering.

The teachings whereby one brings happiness and suffering onto the path can thereby also be understood.

In that way, if you understand how to bring suffering onto the path, then this is the grand finale of suffering. Thus, accordingly, make all faults arise as good qualities. Then suffering will arise as bliss and you will be unharmed by any kind of obstruction or obstacle.

This is why all the sacred forefathers said that happiness and suffering are false. They depend on knowing or not knowing how to change your mind.

We must think that this suffering is the spiritual teacher who points out the shortcomings of cyclic existence and that it is the actual cause of patience and compassion. Moreover, it is that which puts the Dharma practitioner to the test and is a purifier of obscurations. Such ways of regarding suffering as an ornament abound in the biographies of all the past saints.

Furthermore, from Gyalse Togme himself:

> The sign of an excellent Dharma practitioner is that a circumstance of suffering has become an aid for his virtuous practices.

From the teachings of the great Langri Tangpa:

> Because yesterday I felt really badly, my virtuous practice increased.

Moreover, from the teachings of the Dharma Lord Gotsang:

> A Dharma practitioner is clearly distinguished in the face of negative circumstances.

And:

> I was myself inflicted with a great number of fleas; I accepted them for long and took them as my path. Now I am no longer harmed by any suffering.

Moreover, it is said that through the circumstance of illness the great bodhisattva himself gained control over his dreams and increased the activities of virtue.

19

# BRINGING PROSPERITY
# ONTO THE PATH

*Though I may be eminently acclaimed, be revered by many beings,*
*And possess a fortune resembling Vaishravana's,*
*It is the practice of the bodhisattvas to remain without arrogance,*
*Having seen how the glory and riches of this existence are pointless.*

Though I may possess in abundance perfect status, appearance, dominion, and resources, though I am renowned in all directions, though many beings bow their heads toward me with respect and veneration, and though I have obtained wealth and enjoyments similar to King Vaishravana,[24] because I see that all the glory and riches of this existence flicker like lightning, vacillate like dewdrops on the tip of a grass blade, and are as essenceless as a water bubble, and because of realizing that such phenomena are to be discarded like the skin of a snake, I will remain without arrogance and haughtiness. This is the way in which all bodhisattvas bring prosperity onto the path.

From a sutra:

You should not generate a mental state where you think,
"I am especially noble and supremely important."
This infatuation is the root of all carelessness.

*Letter to a Friend* says:

Arrogance based on prestige, beauty, learning, youth, and great authority—behold it as your enemy.

And from *The Way of the Bodhisattva*:

Full of the negative emotion of arrogance,
We will be brought down to the lower realms.

One may be healthy, possess all enjoyments, have perfect qualities in terms of status, appearance, learnedness, and righteousness, and be endowed with vast happiness in body and mind. But if, because of this, one has become arrogant and infatuated with oneself, looks down on others, and falls under the power of wanting to do various non-Dharmic activities, then faults such as carelessness and suffering will be produced in this life. In the next life one will be born in the lower realms, have a lower status, and so forth. In this way, this life and one's future lives entirely degenerate.

*Precious Garland of the Middle Way* states the following:

> Although you may possess perfections similar to a god,
> Do not become arrogant.

From *The Way of the Bodhisattva*:

> In order that I may cause the buddhas' hearts to rejoice,
> I shall from now on be the master of myself and the servant of
>    the world.

Accordingly, whatever mundane or Dharmic excellence occurs, it should become a conducive circumstance for one's practice. Wishing that the same may happen to others, one should immediately transform anything into a means to benefit them. It is taught that one should tame one's arrogance and thereafter behave like the lowest of servants for all, bearing everyone, high or low, on the crown of one's head.

Furthermore, from Lord Atisha:

> Whenever an attitude of superiority appears,
> At that time pride should be humbled.

He continues:

> Condemn all mental states of conceit, vanity, pride, and arrogance;
>    pacify and tame them!
> Give rise to compassion toward all those inferior, and give up
>    disregard and contempt.

Dromtonpa also explained:

> No matter how many qualities you may have,
> Diminish scorn and derision for others.

Potowa explained:

> Bodhisattvas must subdue their pride, keep a low profile, and act
> respectfully and with great compassion toward everyone.
> Even though there were no qualities greater than those of Lord Atisha,
> he never acted with contempt towards anyone, not even a dog.

Moreover:

> If others look at me with pity but I nevertheless remain always
> happy, then there is Dharma in that—otherwise not.

Kharagpa said the following:

> Without seizing the role of the superior,
> Embrace the humble role of an inferior.

As well as:

> Since no qualities whatsoever will arise in a proud person, lower
> your head and remain humble.

Langri Tangpa:

> When accompanying anyone anywhere,
> Regard yourself as inferior to everyone,
> And from the core of your heart
> Respectfully conceive of others as paramount.

In the same way, all the sacred forefathers taught through their lifestyles how to practice the Dharma by means of taking a low seat, wearing tattered clothes, and so forth.

Moreover, it is said:

> If you are happy, dedicate it toward a joyful assembly.

These statements also demonstrate the manner of bringing suffering and happiness onto the path.

There is an expression, "This is the great joyful oppression," which means that if one knows how to bring happiness onto the path, the occurrence of happiness and bliss will not become the cause for arrogance and so forth. It will become the oppressor of arrogance and a helper for the Dharma.

Furthermore, from Gyalse Togme himself:

> Also, whatever qualities of learnedness, righteousness, and excellence we Dharma practitioners may possess, if we regard ourselves as paramount and, based on pride, look down on those inferior to us, compete with those equal to us, and begrudge our superiors, then the Dharma has not penetrated to the vital point.

Moreover:

> Therefore, it matters not where or with whom you keep company.
> Carry your superiors, your equals, and those below you on the crown of your head.

He himself practiced in that way.

In short, what is necessary to understand is that whatever appears—whether prosperity, decline, happiness, or suffering—is like an illusion, and so when happy, be able to cope with happiness, and when sad, be able to cope with suffering. Otherwise, when slight happiness occurs, one becomes arrogant, and when slight suffering occurs, one becomes discouraged and disheartened. Nothing will be accomplished by such a weakling.

Potowa said the following:

> Though you may have circled the town ten times and still have not received any alms, do not become discouraged.
> Though reverence may fall like rain, do not become happy and attached.

Chekawa explained:

> Be patient, whether there is decline or prosperity.

Then, from *Ornament of the Sutras*:

> At the time of prosperity and at the time of decline,
> There is no fear of afflictions and suffering.

Thus, one should train to become just like that.

# BRINGING THE OBJECT OF
# AVERSION ONTO THE PATH

*If I do not tame the enemy that is my own anger,*
*Subduing outer enemies will only increase them.*
*Therefore, it is the practice of bodhisattvas to tame one's own being*
*By means of the armies of loving-kindness and compassion.*

Among all enemies, the most difficult to tame are the ferocious enemies of
the negative emotions, such as anger, within our stream-of-being. If we manage to tame them, then just as smoke vanishes when a fire is extinguished, all
outer enemies and demons will, of their own accord, become automatically
pacified. Yet if we do not subdue them, then however many of the outer, ordinary, trouble-making enemies we may conquer, it is the nature of things that
they will not be depleted but will instead increase.

Therefore, to tame the negative emotions in one's being with antidotes
that uproot and subdue them, such as the great army of love that wishes all
enemies and friends to be endowed with happiness and that of compassion
that wishes them to be free of all suffering, is the practice whereby all bodhisattvas bring an object of aversion onto the path.

From *The Way of the Bodhisattva*:

> Unruly sentient beings are as unlimited as space;
> Never will they all be overcome.
> However, if this angry mind alone is subdued,
> Every enemy will thereby be destroyed.

Also:

> Where could we find such amounts of leather
> To cover the whole earth with leather!

Yet by simply wrapping some leather around your feet
It's as if the whole earth has been covered.

Accordingly, if we do not tame the enemies within our own being, we may tame outer enemies, but there will be no end to them. It furthermore teaches:

By simply binding this mind alone,
All these things are likewise bound.
By simply taming this mind alone,
All these things are likewise tamed.

Thus, if we tame our own mindstream, it is the same as taming all enemies. From the *Hundred Verses*:

Even though the harmful has been slain,
The enemy will not come to an end.
If one's own anger is killed,
Through that, all enemies are slain.

*The Treasure of Precious Well-Spoken Statements* also explains it accordingly.

There are many methods for taming the mind, although here cultivation of love and compassion is taught. These two, love and compassion, are the highway of the Great Vehicle and the root of the mind of enlightenment.

*Ornament of the Sutras* states:

Its root is considered to be compassion.

And:

Love is the stem for compassion.

From *Precious Garland of the Middle Way*:

That Great Vehicle, which explains
That all conduct is to be preceded by compassion and
Embraced with stainless wisdom—
Who, of sound mind, would look down on that?

*Entering into the Middle Way* states:

Love is the perfect harvest of the victorious ones;
Indeed, it is considered the seed, the enriching water,
And the ripening, remaining as enjoyment for long.
Therefore, I shall praise compassion first of all.

Furthermore, Lord Atisha explained:

> If the inner mind is tamed,
> An outer enemy cannot cause harm.

He continued:

> If you lack love and compassion, you are not a bodhisattva.

And:

> Tibetans might know of some bodhisattvas who have no idea how to train in love and compassion. Well then, what should they do? They should train gradually from the beginning.

Dromtonpa also said:

> If one never parts from loving-kindness, compassion, and the mind of enlightenment, rebirth in the lower realms will be impossible. Therefore, this is known as instantly becoming a nonreturner.

Potowa exclaimed:

> Since we will not become enlightened through apprehending an enemy and conceptualizing in terms of near and far, we must give rise to an impartial loving-kindness toward all sentient beings equal to the limits of space.

Kharagpa explained the following:

> Give up all malice and ill will
> Toward all kind sentient beings of the three realms
> Who, in the past, were your parents,
> And thus meditate on loving-kindness.

When Chen-ngawa was explaining many reasons why loving-kindness is so important, Langri Tangpa prostrated to him and said, "From today on, I will cultivate loving-kindness exclusively." Chen-ngawa took off his hat and, after folding his hands above his head, said, "This is extremely wondrous!"

Once the three brothers, Puchungwa, Chen-ngawa, and Potowa, along with a disciple of Khamlungpa, went to meet Dromtonpa. Potowa and the others inquired about Dromtonpa's doings, and in the end, Drom inquired, "Khamlungpa, what has he been doing?" They answered, "He has seated himself at the bank of a river, has covered his head, and does nothing but cry." Drom took off his hat, folded his hands, and after shedding a few tears, exclaimed, "How extremely wondrous!" Praising Khamlungpa's meditation on compassion, he said: "If we could also give rise to such an unfabricated loving-kindness, then we would be able to directly exchange the happiness and suffering of ourselves and others and, without any concern for our life and body, be able to accomplish the benefit of others."

Furthermore, from the bodhisattva himself:

> You should give up the mind hostile toward the enemy. If you do not subdue your anger, the outer enemies will not disappear through conquests. If you tame that, it will not be necessary to conquer enemies.

Moreover:

> If we lack the intention to liberate beings equal to space,
> Perfect enlightenment will not be achieved.
> Therefore, we should cultivate love and great compassion.

He taught in that way and practiced exactly that.

21

# BRINGING THE OBJECT OF
# ATTACHMENT ONTO THE PATH

*Sense pleasures are like salty water;*
*However much one partakes of them, craving will only increase.*
*Hence, it is the practice of bodhisattvas to abandon immediately*
*All objects that generate attachment.*

Even if one obtains desirable objects—forms, sounds, fragrances, flavors, and textures, endowed with beautiful and pleasing, sweet and delicious, or smooth and lovely qualities resembling the enjoyments of the god Indra—it is just as if one has drunk salty water. However much one makes use of them, one never feels satisfied or fulfilled. Craving and suffering will only increase further. Because of this, attachment to the cornucopia of samsara is the source of numerous shortcomings now and in future lives.

Therefore, one should generally not become attached to any material enjoyment, and in particular to any kind of attractive belongings and necessities, large or small. Rather, without letting any time lapse, one must give up such enjoyments and objects and abandon them immediately in order to stop clinging and attachment. This is the manner of practice whereby all bodhisattvas bring an object of attachment onto the path.

From the *Sutra of the Great Display*:

Sense pleasures create great misery and harm;
They bring terror, perpetual enmity, and negative emotions.
They are like the sharp edge of a knife and are equal to the leaves of a
  poisonous plant.
Like a vessel of vomit, they are discarded by the noble ones.

As well as:

> Delighting in sense pleasures will,
> Like drinking salt water, never be satisfying.

Thus, it is taught that the shortcomings of sense pleasures abound.
In *Purposeful Expressions* it is said:

> Even if it may rain with *karshapana* coins,
> The desirous ones will not be satisfied.
> That all desires are petty and full of faults,
> All the wise ones have understood.

The *Sutra Requested by Narayana* also teaches that whatever one feels attachment for and cannot let go of must be given up.
*Letter to a Friend* teaches:

> All desires yield devastation.

And *The Way of the Bodhisattva* repeatedly makes statements such as:

> In this world and in the ones to come,
> All desires cause destruction.

All these point out the shortcomings of attachment to sense objects in general. The many defects of specific attachments to glory, alcohol, women, wealth, and commodities are also explained but will not be elaborated here.

To diminish one's attachment and so train in having only a few desires and being content is praised as supreme. Concerning this, it is said in *Letter to a Friend*:

> The teacher of gods and humans has taught
> That among all riches, contentment is the most supreme.

In *The Way of the Bodhisattva*, it is said:

> The blissful enjoyment of contentment
> Is difficult even for Lord Indra to find.

Also:

> That which is not perceived as attractive—
> That is an excellent object.

Thus, it is praiseworthy to immediately reject objects that engender clinging and attachment.

Furthermore, Lord Atisha said:

> Attachment to anything whatsoever should be abandoned;
> One should remain free from attachments.
> Because of attachment, the blissful realms are not attained;
> Attachment also cuts through the life force of liberation.

And:

> Dear friends, all sense pleasures are like drinking salty water—
> you will never feel satisfied. Therefore, please be content.

And:

> The supreme sign of success is that desires diminish.

Puchungwa also explained:

> The happiness that comes from abandoning desire is more in-
> tense than the one that is based on desire.

Potowa explained:

> Because of yearning after pleasures without ever feeling satisfied,
> there is nothing to experience but the suffering of the lower realms
> and samsara.

Kharagpa said the following:

> Desire does not allow you to rise above samsara. Therefore, if you
> do not regard desire as a fault, you will have gone astray.

Nambarwa said:

> If you do not forcefully cut through attachment, the lure of sense
> pleasures will remain intact. Therefore, cast away the things you
> own, like spitting in the dirt.

Nyugrumpa taught:

> You should give rise to the notion of sense pleasures as a ground
> of burning embers.

Shabopa also explained:

> If you do not turn your mind away from desires, there will be no way to find happiness in this life and in the next. If you turn your mind away from desires, you will not need to look for happiness.

And:

> When you are able to reverse the manifold desirous states of mind, this then is the onset of happiness.

Furthermore, from the bodhisattva himself:

> If you are attached to wealth, property, relatives, retinue, servants, and so forth,
> You are like an elephant sinking into the mud.

And:

> If your mind is simply content with whatever you possess,
> Then your body will be relaxed and your mind blissful, while study, reflection, and meditation will increase.
> When free from the torment of hoarding, guarding, and losing
> And endowed with contentment, then even a beggar is rich.

In this way, Gyalse Togme himself trained in having few desires and being content.

## 22

## TRAINING IN SIMPLICITY FREE
## FROM FIXATION DURING
## MEDITATIVE EQUIPOISE

*Whatever appears is all one's own mind;*
*Mind itself is primordially beyond all mental constructs.*
*Knowing this, it is the practice of the bodhisattvas*
*Not to hold on to any attributes of perceiver and perceived.*

No matter how all these outer and inner phenomena appear, the vessel
and its contents are mere imputations of our own mind, empty of any existence of their own. Even the imputing mind itself is primordially free from
all extremes such as existence and nonexistence, eternalism and nihilism. In this
way, one understands the ultimate real condition of all phenomena subsumed
under subject and object, exactly as it is. To meditate on emptiness, free of
mental constructs, without dwelling on any attributes—such as believing that
there is any true existence to the outer perceived object and the inner perceiving mind—is the manner of practice whereby bodhisattvas cultivate resting in the equanimity of spacelike emptiness.

From the *Prajnaparamita Sutra:*

> Complete knowledge of the manner in which all phenomena are
> unborn and empty
> Is supreme engagement in transcendent knowledge.

And also:

> The meditation of transcendent knowledge is not to meditate on
> anything whatsoever.

And also:

> Meditation of transcendent knowledge is a meditation of space.

118

Accordingly, no phenomena, subsumed under the category of "external objects," exist apart from being mere imputations of mind. Since the imputing mind itself is also beyond arising, dwelling, and ceasing, all phenomena, which appear as "the perceiver and the perceived," remain as emptiness free from mental constructs. When a yogi has gained certainty regarding the natural state in this way, he rests undistractedly in a state of not mentally engaging in anything at all. Here the outer perceived object does not exist as anything whatsoever, the perceiving mind does not grasp at anything whatsoever—entity or nonentity, etc.—and nothing whatsoever is conceptualized. This is the manner of meditating in the equanimity of spacelike emptiness.

From *Commentary on the Enlightened Mind*:

> A mind free of focus
> Dwells in the characteristic of space.
> This meditation of space
> Is asserted to be meditation on emptiness.

In *The Way of the Bodhisattva*, it is said:

> Whenever entities and nonentities
> Do not dwell before your mind,
> Since at that time there are no other features,
> Absence of a reference point is utter peace.

Thus, also:

> Everything is like space.
> All of you, who are like me, must comprehend this thoroughly.

Moreover, Lord Atisha explained:

> Within intrinsic nature free of mental constructs,
> Leave also the mind free from mental constructs!

And:

> Realizing by way of nonconception
> Is termed "realization of the ultimate."

Dromtonpa also said the following:

> The natural state, empty of the three times,
> Is not to be sought outside, for you will be deceived by the object.

It is not to be sought inside, for you will be deceived by yourself.
•The knowledge of these two as nonexistent is not to be sought.

Potowa said:

During composure, meditate, in the manner of not conceiving
of anything, on all phenomena as being empty and without self-
nature, like the center of space.

Kharagpa explained:

Since the natural state does not exist as anything whatsoever,
It is naturally free of the four extremes.
Since the mind does not conceptualize anything,
Be free of grasping thoughts.

Sharawa exclaimed:

When you have become certain that all things are like space,
without any essence whatsoever and free from extremes, then
in this state do not conceive of, or grasp at, anything. Thus, having given up all thoughts and mental doing, one should remain
one-pointedly in the state of emptiness.

Langri Tangpa said:

All of that must not be polluted
By the stains of the eight extremes.

He taught that one should meditate free of mental constructs, unpolluted by
the stains of conceptual thoughts, which fixate on phenomena as being established in the manner of any of the eight extremes.
    Chekawa:

Think that all phenomena are like a dream,
Investigate the nature of unborn awareness.
Let even the antidote be liberated by itself;
Rest in the state of the all-ground, the essence of the path.

Hence, it is explained that meditation on the ultimate mind of enlightenment occurs when, having resolved that the outer object, the inner mind, and
the concept of the antidote are all emptiness, one lets go within that state.

Furthermore, from Gyalse Togme himself:

> Since the natural state of all knowables is beyond concepts,
> One gives up mental fabrications, such as being or not being,
> And remains one-pointedly in the state free of mental constructs.
> This is meditation on the ultimate mind of enlightenment.

And he continued, "Rest undistractedly in the state free of mental constructs." He taught that and practiced accordingly.

## 23

# GIVING UP FIXATION ON THE
# OBJECT OF ATTACHMENT
# AS BEING REAL

*When encountering a beautiful object,*
*One should consider it to be like a rainbow in summertime:*
*It appears attractive yet is not thought to be truly existent.*
*To so give up attachment is the practice of the bodhisattvas.*

When encountering delightful objects such as one's friends, exquisite forms, pleasant sounds, happiness, those who are happy, and so forth, such appearances are like the summertime rainbow, which appears beautifully and vividly yet does not exist the way it appears. Accordingly, one regards these ravishing and beautiful appearances as unreal and one does not apprehend them as having any kind of true existence, thinking, "This is my friend, this is my relative, this is beautiful, and this is dear to me." To give up such attachment and fixation on a true and concrete reality of those is the manner of practice whereby all bodhisattvas stop their fixation on objects of attachment as being real.

24

GIVING UP FIXATION

ON THE OBJECT OF AVERSION

AS BEING REAL

*The various sufferings are just like the death of one's child in a dream;*
*How very tiring to grasp illusory appearances as being real!*
*Therefore, when encountering adverse circumstances,*
*It is the practice of bodhisattvas to regard them as illusions.*

When various undesirable objects, such as repulsive enemies and demons, ugly forms, unpleasant sounds, suffering, and those who suffer, appear to your mind, such appearances are just like the suffering one experiences while dreaming of the death of one's child. Holding on to confused appearances, such as pain being real, one becomes weary and exhausted and so suffers. Therefore, when meeting with unfavorable and unpleasant circumstances, one does not fixate on them as being real, thinking, "This is an enemy! This is awful!" One regards them all with the thought, "Apart from being mere delusive appearances, they have no real existence of their own." Such is the manner of practice whereby all bodhisattvas stop their fixation on an object of aversion as being real.

In this way both the previous stanza as well as this one show how, having stopped fixation on objects that produce attachment and aversion as being real during post-meditation, one meditates on such objects as resembling a rainbow in the sky, a dream, and an illusion.

One can explain the meaning by quoting the *King of Samadhi Sutra*:

Magicians create illusory forms
Of horses, elephants, chariots, and various kinds.
Despite their appearance, they have no existence whatsoever.
Understand all phenomena to be like that.

When a young girl sees in her dream
The birth of her son and also his death,
She feels joy at his birth and grief at his death.
Understand all phenomena to be like that.

Even though phenomena such as forms are not real, they appear distinctly, just like illusory horses, elephants, and dream appearances.

Moreover, from *The Way of the Bodhisattva*:

How can that which confusion takes for truth
In any way be different from illusion?

Like the death of one's child in a dream,
The concept that thinks it is no more
Is an obstruction for the concept that thinks it still is,
Yet this concept also is false.

In this regard, if at the time of meditative composure the meditation on emptiness is very intense, then at the post-meditation stage all appearances will spontaneously appear as illusory and dreamlike. If the realization during meditative composure is modest, then during the post-meditation stage one must rely upon deliberate mindfulness, thinking, "Whatever appears is untrue, like an illusion." Not only that, but through meditating on emptiness, one acquires, during the occasion of post-meditation, compassion for sentient beings and confidence in cause and effect, and by that one will spontaneously engage in the accumulation of merit.

Moreover, from Lord Atisha:

When an object of aversion or attachment appears,
Regard it as a magical illusion.

Potowa also explained:

All phenomena as they appear during post-meditation to our confused minds are like an illusion and a dream. You should act like a magician, without any attached fixation on them!

Sharawa said:

When rising from meditative composure, one practices all virtues, such as generosity, embraced by wisdom and great compassion, and so one mainly trains in the accumulation of merit.

Kharagpa:

> All phenomena are like dreams and illusions;
> There is nothing that is true,
> For things appear although they are nonexistent.
> Do not have great attachment to them as real.

> While not existing in the natural state,
> They are like causes and effects in a dream.
> Since the illusory effects of karma are unfailing,
> Give up evil and put all your force into virtue.

Langri Tangpa explained:

> By understanding all phenomena as illusions,
> Liberate yourself from the fetters of attachment.

Rinchen Gangpa said:

> When fettered by the shackles of fixation on reality,
> The ground of the two accumulations cannot be covered.
> Though phenomena appear, be free of attachment;
> They are just like an illusion—how important that is!

Chekawa said:

> In between sessions, act as an illusory being.

It is taught that no matter what one does during post-meditation, one must, without departing from the experience of meditative composure, understand oneself to be as unreal as an illusory being. These examples demonstrate the manner of illusionlike meditation during post-meditation.

Furthermore, from Gyalse Togme himself:

> In post-meditation, all appearances are like an illusion.
> With the understanding that even though they appear, they are
>     not real,
> To benefit others from this state of nonfixation
> Is the post-meditation practice of the ultimate mind of enlightenment.

He continues:

> In post-meditation, however the relative may manifest,
> From within the state of knowing that, despite its appearance, it is
>    not real,
> Let your three doors fully endeavor in the ten virtues.

He taught this and put it into practice accordingly.

25

TRAINING IN GENEROSITY

*If, when wishing for enlightenment, one must give up even one's body,*
*So giving up external objects goes without question!*
*Therefore, it is the practice of the bodhisattvas to be generous*
*Without any hope for reward or positive result.*

Just as it is taught in stories of the Buddha's past lives, when wishing to attain the level of a perfect buddha, the great enlightenment, one must repeatedly give away one's limbs or head or even one's whole body to benefit others. Needless it is then to say that one must give away such things as one's outer wealth, enjoyments, children, spouse, and so forth to others. It is therefore necessary to train in the practice of generosity.

Regarding that, one grants the three kinds of generosity, along with the roots of virtue and their results, to others, embracing this with an extraordinarily generous attitude. One does so free of hope for one's own benefit in this life, such as expecting to get food, wealth, and so forth in return. Likewise, one does so not striving for any karmic ripening that is to occur in the form of great enjoyments in a future life. Such is the practice whereby bodhisattvas train in the paramita of generosity.

Moreover, from *Entering into the Middle Way*:

The paramita of generosity constitutes the ability to give.

*The Way of the Bodhisattva* states:

Mentally giving away to all beings
All one's possessions, together with the result,
Is said to be the paramita of generosity.

Thus, the essence of generosity is the virtue of a generous attitude and the actions of body and speech fully motivated by this attitude.

Furthermore, correctly giving outer and inner things is the first of the three kinds of generosity, the generosity of material goods. Protecting all sentient beings from the fears of mankind, of nonhumans, and of the elements is the second, the generosity of fearlessness. To teach, unmistakenly, the holy Dharma and to point out and instruct others in wholesome worldly livelihood is the third, the generosity of the Dharma.

As to the manner of giving rise to a generous attitude, it says in *The Way of the Bodhisattva*:

> My body and likewise my enjoyments
> As well as my virtues of the three times
> I shall give away without any sense of loss
> To bring about the benefit of beings.

The support for one's conduct—meditation on the mind of enlightenment and making aspirational prayers toward enlightenment—is the root of all giving and is taught to be supreme. This also is the case in terms of the other paramitas.

Concerning the faults of keeping and the qualities of giving, *The Paramita Compendium* states:

> Through giving, one will not be overpowered by negative emotions.
> Miserliness is not the noble path but the creator of negative emotions;
> Generosity is the supreme path.
> Anything other than that is said to be below the noble path.

Concerning this, there are many other statements.

As for having no hope for reward or ripening, *Ornament of the Sutras* mentions "the generosity that is without expectations," which is said to be the extraordinary way of practicing generosity.

Moreover, Lord Atisha explained:

> Since these impermanent enjoyments are pointless, practice generosity adorned with excellent qualities.

And he continued in this way:

> The supreme generosity is nonattachment.

Gonpawa also said:

> The root of generosity comes down to nonattachment.

And from Potowa:

> Through the habituation of training in giving away the trivial, such as a needle and thread, one will come to be able to give away anything without attachment.

Moreover:

> Who would cut off one's ear and attach it to one's butt? Likewise, do not for the sake of generosity cut away flesh from the thigh of your discipline.

In accordance with the above, Sharawa said:

> I will not explain to you the benefits of generosity, but I will explain to you the shortcomings of miserliness.

Since virtue will thereby not decrease but will instead be acquired without any hardship, it is taught that ordained ones, too, should practice material generosity. Furthermore, from Gyalse Togme himself:

> The Sage has praised generosity that is free from expectations
> Of gaining anything in return in this life or of karmic ripening
>     in future lives.

Also:

> May I, when seeing one in need, give rise to delight,
> And with a smiling, friendly countenance,
> Give away—with a mind free of any hope—whatever is desired:
> My enjoyments, even my own body, my life, my flesh and blood.

Thus, he made aspirational prayers to train in the three kinds of generosity and practiced accordingly.

# 26

# TRAINING IN DISCIPLINE

*Lacking discipline, one will not accomplish one's own benefit,*
*And so the wish to accomplish the benefit of others will be laughable.*
*Therefore, it is the practice of the bodhisattvas to observe discipline*
*Free of any mundane ambitions.*

If, when not keeping one's avowed discipline completely pure, one is not only unable to accomplish the higher realms for one's own benefit but is in fact on the way to the lower realms, then the wish to accomplish perfect enlightenment for the benefit of others is indeed a laughable one.

One must not be involved with pursuing the support of a rebirth in the higher realms, divine or human, because of attachment to existence or because of mundane cravings. Carefully observing the three types of discipline with a mind focused on accomplishing perfect enlightenment for the benefit of others is the manner of practice whereby all bodhisattvas train in the paramita of discipline.

Furthermore, from *Precious Garland of the Middle Way*:

> Discipline is the act of benefiting others.

*The Way of the Bodhisattva* states:

> The achievement of the mind of renunciation
> Is explained as the paramita of discipline.

The essence of discipline is an attitude of renunciation that turns the mind away from harming others, along with the basis for that.

The pledge to refrain from all inherent and ethical unwholesomeness of whatever kind is the first of the three types of discipline, the discipline of resolve.

To give rise to virtuous qualities, such as the six paramitas that have not yet arisen in one's stream-of-being, and to prevent those that have already

130

arisen from diminishing and instead increase them further is the second type, the discipline of gathering virtuous qualities.

To accomplish, through any suitable means free from impropriety, the benefit of all sentient beings in this and future lives is the third type, the discipline that acts for the welfare of sentient beings.

When the essence of discipline is posited as renunciation, it is in terms of the discipline of resolve. This is mainly concerned with giving up all natural wrongdoing. Again this means primarily giving up the ten nonvirtues. Therefore, one must correctly discipline oneself so that one does not stray even on the level of intention.

The identification of all the trainings in the bodhichittas of aspiration and application, as well as the root and branch downfalls, will not be elaborated upon in this text.

Concerning the faults of degenerated discipline, the following is said in the *Prajnaparamita Sutra*:

> When, due to a corrupted discipline, one is unable to accomplish
> even one's own benefit, what is left to say about benefiting others?
> The full ripening of debased discipline is the realm of hell beings
> or animals or the realm of the Lord of Death.

*The Paramita Compendium* states:

> If, when allowing one's discipline to degenerate, one cannot
>     accomplish one's own benefit,
> From where will the power to benefit others then come?

There are many statements similar to this one. As for the advantages of observing discipline, *Letter to a Friend* states:

> Just as the earth is the basis for the animate and the inanimate,
> Discipline is taught to be the basis for all good qualities.

Other statements similar to this one abound.

Concerning the root stanza "free of any mundane ambitions," *Ornament of the Sutras* mentions "the discipline free of craving for rebirth."

Hence, it teaches how to practice the extraordinary discipline that becomes the cause for liberation and omniscient wisdom.

Furthermore, from Lord Atisha:

> It brings splendor in this life and happiness in the next, so always
> observe all disciplines purely.

Also:

> Observe the discipline of seeking to accept and reject correctly,
> The ground from which all qualities appear.

And:

> The best kind of discipline is a mind at peace.

Gonpawa also said:

> The root of discipline comes down to following a spiritual friend.

Potowa explained:

> The basis for all excellent qualities is the discipline of resolve and
> the samayas. Therefore, if one is lacking discipline or if the samayas
> are not pure, that will become an obstacle to developing qualities
> and to all accomplishments.

More:

> In order to keep discipline pure, one should not be attached to
> the pleasures of the three times.

Kharagpa said:

> The cause for obtaining the human body of freedom and riches
> Is the precious training in discipline;
> Observe it in your being as much as you can,
> Purely and without stains.

Jayulwa:

> Fully observe the pure discipline, for it is the basis for the path to
> liberation and omniscience.

Khamlungpa explained the following:

> When famine occurs, everything depends on barley. In the same
> way, since everything depends on discipline, apply yourself to it.
> Also, without reflecting on the effects of actions, a pure discipline
> will not come about. Therefore, this reflection is oral instruction.

Sharawa said:

> One generally relies on the Dharma, no matter what may happen. If one relies accurately on the teachings of the Vinaya, one won't need to add anything: one's heart will be pure, one's discernment stable, one will be delighted, and in the end everything will be excellent.

These statements teach that the root of all qualities is discipline; that for the purpose of keeping this discipline pure, one must rely on excellent friends; that one must give up desires and reflect on the effects of karma; and that one must act in accordance with the Vinaya, accept and reject in a very meticulous way, and so forth.

Furthermore, Gyalse Togme himself said:

> Since discipline is the basis for all qualities,
> Forsake injury to others as though it were poison.

Also:

> Having realized that the trainings of the bliss-gone ones are more
>     precious than even my life,
> May I through mindfulness and carefulness abide
> And establish others within a discipline that is unstained, even for
>     an instant,
> By faults, downfalls, and defilements.

He himself aspired to train in the three kinds of discipline, and he put them into practice accordingly.

27

## TRAINING IN PATIENCE

*For a bodhisattva who wishes for the enjoyments of virtue,*
*All harm-doers are like precious treasures.*
*Therefore, it is the practice of bodhisattvas to cultivate patience,*
*Free of hatred and animosity toward anyone.*

The great vast enjoyment of virtue—the meditation on patience—is supreme among all austerity practices. For all bodhisattvas who wish to engage in such practice, all harm that appears, such as suffering and enemies, is like opening up an inexhaustible treasure of priceless wish-fulfilling jewels, rare to find, within their own house. Hence, to meditate on the three kinds of patience, without having even the slightest angry or hateful thought toward those who are causing harm, is the practice whereby all bodhisattvas train in the paramita of patience.

*Ornament of the Sutras* mentions "the patient endurance of taking no offense." And *Precious Garland of the Middle Way* teaches:

Patience is the abandonment of anger.

Taking no offense toward those who cause harm, joyfully accepting suffering when it occurs, and remaining extremely interested in becoming certain about the Dharma are the essence of patience.

Not to feel disturbed by harm-doers is the patience of taking no offense toward those who cause harm. If suffering occurs, not to feel disturbed and discouraged is the patience of joyfully accepting suffering. Having found certainty in the nature of the qualities of the Three Jewels and in the meaning of selflessness, one reflects again and again until these two do not constitute any conflict. This is the patience of understanding the Dharma.

As for the faults of anger, the faults that are not visible in the present life are described in the *Bodhisattva Pitaka*:

That which is called anger destroys the roots of virtue accumulated over a hundred thousand eons.

In *The Way of the Bodhisattva* it is said:

Any virtue accumulated for a thousand eons,
Such as generosity and offerings to the buddhas;
All of it will be utterly destroyed
By a single moment of anger.

As for the faults that are visible, such as not being able to experience a peaceful mind in this life, the same source states:

When having painful, angry thoughts,
The mind will not experience peace.

Concerning the benefits of patience, it states:

One who is disciplined will conquer anger;
He will be happy in this life and in the ones to come.

Hence, there are many ultimate and temporary benefits: happiness in the present as well as in future lives, not falling into the lower realms, the attainment of the higher realms, liberation, and so forth.

Just as the root verses directly point out, it is not enough to simply refrain from being angry at the harm-doer. It is reasonable to be happy about them, just as when finding precious treasure. As for that, *The Way of the Bodhisattva* says the following:

If I had not caused him harm,
This one would inflict no harm on me.
Rather it is like a treasure appearing in my house
Without my having applied any effort.

Those ways of bringing bad circumstances onto the path that were explained before are all included here in the practice of patience.

As for "Free of hatred and animosity toward anyone," *Ornament of the Sutras* mentions, "Be patient toward everything." Hence, it teaches how to practice the extraordinary patience of bearing with everything, such as suffering and harm-doers.

Furthermore, Lord Atisha said the following:

> In the dark age anger will be rampant; therefore, wear the armor of patience free of anger.

He continues:

> The supreme patience is to take a low seat.

In *The Questions and Answers of the Father Teachings* appears:

> Atisha, if harm is inflicted, how shall I take it?
> Drom, do not return anyone's rage.
> Atisha, if I am (about) to be killed, how shall I take that?
> Drom, you must understand it to be the response to your having killed in the past.

Gonpawa also explained:

> The root of patience comes down to being humble.

Chen-ngawa said the following:

> If you are not patient and so go off to return harm to the harm-doer, then having done that, there will be no end to harm. When this is the case, nothing good will occur. Therefore, you need to be patient in order to be successful in the Dharma.

Potowa said:

> If one fails to cultivate patience when just slight harm occurs, then one loses one's vows and thereby destroys the teachings from their root. We are not universal masters of the teachings. But if we lose our vows, then our purpose has vanished.

Kharagpa explained:

> Since anger is that which conquers virtue from its root, not to regard it as a fault would be a mistake.

Chekawa said the following:

> Do not hold on to things too long, and do not lie in ambush.

Hence, if you have held a grudge toward others for the harm they've created, do not attack even when an opportunity opens up for you to retaliate.

Furthermore, Gyalse Togme himself states:

> Since the enemy, anger, steals the splendor of this and future lives,
> A great army of patience is extremely important.

He continues in this way:

> If one tames one's crude mind, one is the ultimate hero;
> If one tames the enemy of anger, one is the ultimate victor.

And:

> Even if beings blazing with the fire of anger
> Crush my head or slice my body with their weapons,
> May their bonfire of evil and suffering become pacified
> Through the strength of compassion.

In this way he himself made aspirational prayers to practice the three kinds of patience, and he likewise practiced them.

# 28

# TRAINING IN DILIGENCE

*Even the shravakas and pratyekabuddhas, who accomplish only*
*their own benefit,*
*Are seen to be as persistent as those extinguishing a fire*
*burning in their hair.*
*It is the practice of the bodhisattvas to muster diligence,*
*The source of all qualities, for the benefit of all beings.*

Shravakas and pratyekabuddhas wish to accomplish mere peace and happiness for nothing but their own benefit. When they train on the path, they are seen to engage with a diligence so intense that it is likened to the endeavors of someone who in an emergency extinguishes a flame that has ignited his hair or clothes. Having given rise to a mind that aspires to supreme enlightenment for the benefit of beings, one trains in the various vast and difficult conducts of the bodhisattvas. Thus, it is needless to mention that one must engage with a similar vast sense of diligence—the source of all good qualities. Therefore, to train in the three kinds of diligence in order to accomplish perfect enlightenment is the practice whereby bodhisattvas train in the paramita of diligence.

From *Precious Garland of the Middle Way*:

Diligence is indeed to be fond of virtue.

*The Way of the Bodhisattva* also explains, "Diligence means being fond of virtue." The essence of diligence is to be fully delighted when focusing on the object of virtue.

Moreover, all bodhisattvas muster diligence in three ways: The first, armor-like diligence, means joyfully donning the great armor of courage. The second, the diligence of gathering virtuous properties, is to apply oneself to authentically accomplishing the virtue of the paramitas and so forth. The third, the diligence of benefiting sentient beings, is to benefit sentient beings in any way that is free from evil.

In *Ornament of the Sutras* and in the *Abhidharma Treasury*, five kinds of diligence are explained.

As to the faults of refraining from being diligent, the *Sutra of the Application of Mindfulness* states the following:

> The sole basis for all negative emotions
> Is laziness; whoever is lazy,
> That indolent one,
> Lacks all virtuous properties.

Hence, if one lacks diligence, having fallen under the power of laziness, one is deprived of all virtuous properties. All benefit in this life and in the future will thereby degenerate.

Concerning the benefits of diligence, *Ornament of the Sutras* states the following:

> Among the gathering of goodness, diligence is supreme;
> Based on it, qualities are attained.

There are many statements that speak in this way.

In *Entering into the Middle Way* as well it is said:

> All qualities follow diligence without exception.

From *The Way of the Bodhisattva*:

> Thus patiently I shall persevere in diligence,
> For those who exert themselves will find enlightenment.

Such statements abound.

If all shravakas and pratyekabuddhas, who are only accomplishing their own welfare, need to engage very strongly in diligence, then it is reasonable for all bodhisattvas to engage in a diligence that is even a hundred times greater. Concerning this, we have the following statement from *Ornament of the Sutras*:

> Carrying the great burden of sentient beings on his head,
> It is not fitting for a great bodhisattva to move about leisurely.
> Since I and others are bound tightly by fetters,
> It is appropriate to increase diligence a hundred times.

As for "the source of all qualities," *Ornament of the Sutras* mentions that "the source of all qualities is diligence." So it teaches how to accomplish the extraordinary diligence from which all mundane and supramundane qualities appear.

Moreover, Lord Atisha said the following:

> Because of laziness we are still left behind, so kindle the diligence of practice like fire.

He continues:

> No heroes are harmed by the enemy;
> All diligent ones are free from obstacles.

As well as:

> The supreme diligence is to give up negative actions.

Gonpawa explained:

> The root of diligence comes down to the contemplation of death.

Potowa spoke the following:

> In order to accomplish enlightenment, we ordinary beings need to practice for a long time with a diligence that is extremely forceful and uninterrupted.

As well as:

> If impermanence is born in one's being, it becomes the cause for the first type of diligence, which is armorlike.

Kharagpa said:

> Since no good qualities ever appear in someone lacking diligence, meditate on impermanence and give up laziness!

All these statements unanimously teach why it is necessary to muster diligence; how in order to do so one must give up concern for this life; and how for that, again it is necessary to remember death. Furthermore, Gyalse Togme himself taught the following:

> Since through laziness you will accomplish the benefit of neither yourself nor others,
> Give up other activities and endeavor in virtue!

He continues:

Since all virtuous qualities, as many as there are, depend on diligence,
When wishing to accomplish the benefit of oneself and others,
At all times, without ever being distracted,
You should hold diligence as precious as your life.

And:

Accustomed to the idea of establishing
All limitless sentient beings, without exception, in supreme
   enlightenment,
May we remain unmoved by doubts and reservations
Regarding whether or not we will be able to accomplish this goal.

Thus, he himself made aspirational prayers to train in the three kinds of diligence and likewise made them his practice.

# TRAINING IN MEDITATIVE
# CONCENTRATION

*Having understood that clear seeing, fully endowed with peaceful resting,*
*Completely destroys negative emotions,*
*It is the practice of bodhisattvas to cultivate a meditative concentration*
*That truly transcends the four formless realms.*

Clear seeing is the realization of emptiness based on a fully qualified and
perfect peaceful rest that dwells as a one-pointed mind focusing on virtue. It
completely destroys all negative emotions such as ignorance, the source of
samsara, by eliminating them at their very root. Having understood this, one
trains in meditative concentration endowed with extraordinary assistance: great
compassion, which brings an end to the extreme of peace, and clear seeing,
which makes an end to the extreme of existence, etc. Thereby, the mundane
serenities of the four formless realms and so forth, in which peaceful resting
is predominant, will truly be transcended.

To train in such meditative concentrations, which are condensed into three
kinds, is the practice whereby bodhisattvas train in the paramita of meditative
concentration.

Moreover, *Ornament of the Sutras* speaks of "mind resting inwardly," and
*Entering into the Middle Way* mentions "meditative concentration characterized
by composure."

Hence a one-pointed virtuous state of mind that remains undistracted by
other objects is the essence of meditative concentration.

Remaining in meditative equipoise, which is the meditative concentration
of producing pliancy in body and mind, is the first kind of meditative concentration, that of blissful abiding during the present life. The meditative concentration that accomplishes ordinary qualities, such as foreknowledges and
emancipations, is the second, the meditative concentration that fully accom-

plishes qualities. Accomplishing wholesome deeds for the benefit of sentient beings through the power of meditative concentration is the third, the meditative concentration of benefiting sentient beings. These three are distinguished by their different functions, but there are also other ways of making distinctions.

As to the faults of not cultivating meditative concentration, the following is said in *The Way of the Bodhisattva*:

> A person whose mind is completely distracted
> Falls into the fangs of the chasm of negative emotions.

As well as:

> Letting the elephantlike mind run wild
> Will bring us miseries in deepest hell.

In *Letter to a Friend*, it says:

> Without meditative concentration, there will be no knowledge.

Hence, if one lacks meditative concentration, the clear seeing that realizes the lack of self will not arise, and lacking that, the three kinds of enlightenment[25] will not occur.

As to the benefits of meditative concentration, the *Compendium of Trainings* states the following:

> In the authentic and exact meditative composure,
> Understanding will arise; thus the Buddha has taught.

From *The Way of the Bodhisattva*:

> Having understood that clear seeing,
> Fully endowed with peaceful resting,
> Completely destroys all negative emotions,
> Peaceful resting must be sought first.

Hence, based on peaceful rest in which the mind remains in equanimity, clear seeing that authentically sees the natural state will arise, and negative emotions will thereby be abandoned.

This demonstrates the sequence and benefits of peaceful resting and clear seeing.

Concerning the statement "transcends the four formless realms," the following is found in *Ornament of the Sutras*:

Likewise, meditative concentration is not the formless realms.

As their main basis for accomplishing good qualities, bodhisattvas generally practice meditative absorption, comprised of the nine levels of meditative concentration. In particular, they practice the meditative absorption of the fourth meditative concentration,[26] in which the aspects of abidance and clarity are in balance. This is their extraordinary way of practicing meditative absorption.

Lord Atisha said the following:

Since human life runs out on the path of distraction, now is the time when you should remain in meditative composure.

And:

The supreme meditative concentration is an unfabricated mind.

Gonpawa said:

The root of meditative concentration is a place of solitude.

Potowa said the following:

Among people there are many pleasures and lots of things to do. Therefore, virtuous practice does not happen, and therefore, too, meditative concentration will not occur.

As well as:

In order to practice meditative concentration, one needs to have few desires and feel contentment with regard to all outer phenomena.

And:

When not possessing the vows and samayas, one's being will be impure, and therefore, although one meditates, no meditative absorption will arise.

Kharagpa said:

In the mind of a beginner
There is clarity but no stability.
Don't let mind be carried away by the wind of thoughts;
Bind it with the rope of mindfulness.

These statements show that it is reasonable to cultivate meditative absorption and that the supreme meditative absorption is an unfabricated mind.

They also demonstrate that in order to meditate, one must rely on the many types of peaceful rest, and that one must therefore adhere to solitude, give up business, and rely on few desires and on contentment, while observing pure discipline. It is taught that during the main part of practice it is very important to rely on mindfulness.

Moreover, from Gyalse Togme himself:

> Since without meditative concentration the innate nature will not
>    be seen,
> Practice a meditative absorption free of the attributes of conceptuality.

And:

> All appearances are one's own mind.
> The mind itself is primordially free of all extremes.
> Without being distracted by the attributes of perceiver and perceived,
> To remain one-pointedly is the authentic meditative concentration.

Thus, he explained what to be aware of for authentic peaceful rest. Moreover:

> Through the strength of pure meditative concentration
> One attains blissful abidance in the present life.
> Abandoning the experience of this blissful taste,
> May I, through the strength of great compassion,
> Satisfy all beings with the bliss of meditative concentration.

Thus, he aspired to train in the three kinds of meditative concentration and practiced accordingly.

30

# TRAINING IN KNOWLEDGE

*Lacking knowledge, the five other paramitas are not sufficient*
*For the attainment of perfect enlightenment;*
*Hence, it is the practice of bodhisattvas to train in knowledge*
*Endowed with method and beyond conceptions of the three spheres.*

If only the first five paramitas are practiced, they are like a gathering of blind people. In order to attain perfect enlightenment, they must be embraced by the knowledge realizing emptiness—the leader for the blind. Then one is able to progress into the city of omniscient wisdom.

One must therefore cultivate knowledge, which is endowed with vast means—great compassion and the mind of enlightenment—and does not conceptualize the three spheres—the object of meditation, the one who meditates, and the act of meditating—as truly existent. That is the indispensable cause for the attainment of omniscience.

Therefore, to train in the three kinds of knowledge, such as the knowledge that, endowed with the aspect of method, realizes emptiness, is the practice whereby all bodhisattvas train in the paramita of knowledge.

Furthermore, *Ornament of the Sutras* speaks of knowledge as the authentic discernment of all objects of cognition.

Likewise, from the *Abhidharma Compendium*:

What is knowledge? It is the full discernment of all phenomena.

Hence, the essence of knowledge is to clearly distinguish and authentically discern the various phenomena to be examined.

The knowledge of being learned in the five sciences is the first kind of knowledge, that which realizes the relative.

The knowledge that evaluates the meaning of selflessness through its mental image or through its being evident is the second knowledge, that which realizes the ultimate.

To understand how to practice wholesome deeds for the present and future benefit of all sentient beings is the third knowledge, that which realizes what benefits sentient beings.

There are also other ways of classifying knowledge.

As for the faults of lacking knowledge, one will, when so deprived, be unable to accomplish any qualities whatsoever in this life or in future lives. In particular, if one is missing the knowledge that realizes selflessness, the other five paramitas, of generosity and so forth, will be similar to someone who has no eyesight.

From *The Paramita Compendium:*

> When lacking knowledge, the other five paramitas will be blind.
> Without the capacity to see, they will not be able to reach
>   enlightenment.

Concerning the qualities of knowledge, they are the opposite of the faults of lacking knowledge described above, such as being able to accomplish all qualities in this life and in future lives.

From the same source:

> When the five paramitas are embraced by knowledge,
> They gain vision and qualify for their names.[27]

Moreover, the knowledge that realizes emptiness is an important antidote for the two obscurations. This is taught in *The Supreme Continuity* as well as in *The Way of the Bodhisattva.* In this way there are numerous temporary and ultimate benefits of knowledge.

As for the statement "endowed with method," *Ornament of the Sutras* mentions "knowledge endowed with method." Since through mere emptiness one does not progress at all on the path of the Great Vehicle, it teaches that one needs to meditate on that emptiness that, when complete with the aspects of the methods of generosity and so forth, is endowed with all supreme features. This is the extraordinary way of accomplishing knowledge.

These teachings from *Ornament of the Sutras* on how to accomplish the qualities of the six paramitas are the content of the *Sutra Requested by Kashyapa.*

Furthermore, from Lord Atisha:

> Because of wrong views, you have not realized the true meaning.
> Therefore, examine the authentic meaning!

And he continues:

> The one familiar with skillful methods
> Will, by meditating on knowledge,
> Quickly attain enlightenment.

And:

> The supreme knowledge is a total absence of grasping.

He also taught that if one realizes emptiness, the practices of the six paramitas are included in that.

Potowa taught the same. To explain it he quoted the *Paramita Compendium*:

> For those who train in the paramita of knowledge, all paramitas
> are included in that.

Gonpawa explained:

> The root of knowledge comes down to looking into one's mind.

These statements demonstrate how one must meditate on emptiness, how the supreme wisdom is to realize the lack of reality, that both method and knowledge must be complete, and so forth.

Nevertheless, in the beginning, the knowledge that results from studying is most important. Concerning this, Lord Atisha spoke the following:

> Until you have realized the natural state you must study;
> Therefore, listen to the oral instruction of a master!

Naljorpa Chenpo said:

> Lords, in order to accomplish enlightenment we must study as
> many books as a female yak can carry on its back. If we only study
> the amount that can rest on the palms of our hands, we will not
> reach anywhere.

Puchungwa said:

> Open up the books and put them on your pillow since it is our
> job to study. Even if we do not manage to read them, it will still be
> praiseworthy. What is the point of saying that you practice the
> Dharma if you don't know it.

Sharawa explained:

> Until one has become enlightened, there is no end to pursuing
> studies.
> When one has become enlightened, one's studies are over.

Furthermore, from Gyalse Togme himself:

> Without knowledge you will not traverse the path to liberation,
> So gain learning in the profound meaning of the two truths!

And:

> Also the five, of generosity and so forth,
> Depend on knowledge to become paramitas;
> Hence, intending to make all phenomena become the path of
> enlightenment,
> You should train in the paramita of knowledge.

More:

> To accomplish the great purpose with the four meaningful means of
> magnetizing
> And enter into the noble ones' *bhumis,*
> May we, focusing on the relative with the knowledge of devoted
> application,
> Realize perceiver and perceived to be without nature.

Thus, he aspired to train in the three kinds of knowledge and practiced
accordingly.

# 31

# EXAMINING ONE'S CONFUSION,
# SO THAT IT MAY BE DISPELLED

*When not examining one's own confusion,*
*It is possible to have the appearance of a Dharma practitioner*
*    while doing what is not Dharma.*
*Therefore, it is the practice of bodhisattvas to relinquish*
*Their own confusion, through continuously examining it.*

If individuals, such as those who have entered the Great Vehicle, do not repeatedly examine their own confusion and faults at all times, they will lack all qualities such as learnedness and righteousness. Lacking good qualities and, on top of that, not being aware of their faults even though they may be the size of Mount Meru, they will nevertheless think of themselves as being Dharma practitioners.

Also, most others, when looking at their outer appearance, will perceive them as Dharma practitioners because, in effect, they have disguised themselves as such. Under this cover one might engage in non-Dharmic activities such as taming enemies and sustaining friends in this life. Therefore, it is a great fault not to examine one's own faults.

Hence, to examine continuously and carefully the confusion of one's three doors and then to relinquish it is the practice whereby all bodhisattvas give up their own faults through becoming aware of them.

It is said in *Purposeful Expressions*:

I should examine what is appropriate to do and what is not.

From *The Way of the Bodhisattva*:

Checking at all times what am I doing,
In this way should I examine my faults.

It is very important to give up our faults by means of thinking them over and investigating them. In particular, when we ourselves have entered the Great Vehicle, we need to examine our confusion and then give it up so that we may prevent others from losing faith.

In the *Sutra Requested by Inexhaustible Intelligence*, the following is said:

> There is one Dharma that condenses the entire Great Vehicle:
> One must protect all sentient beings through contemplating one's
> own confusion.

More from the *Sutra of the Authentic Compilation of All Phenomena*:

> Protecting others from losing faith means observing discipline.

From *Individual Liberation of the Bodhisattva*:

> Having investigated that which makes the world feel distrust, you
> should eliminate it.

Moreover, from *The Way of the Bodhisattva*:

> When you get rid of your toothbrushes and spittle,
> You should conceal them well.
> Also you are wide of the mark to urinate
> At public places and at water springs.
>
> All such as that, which provokes distrust in this world,
> Should be inquired into and, when observed, abandoned.

The *Compendium of Trainings* mentions that one should "abandon fruitless activity." It continues to teach elaborately on how to give up the factors that prevent benefit and good results for others, as well as the causal factors that may cause others to lose faith. From the same source:

> At all times one who is not wild but gentle
> Will speak at the right time and pleasantly;
> That individual will be liked by all fortunate beings
> Who will fully trust his words.

Therefore, the benefits of having examined one's own faults and abandoned them are that others develop faith and trust your words.

Furthermore, as to the faults of provoking distrust in others, the following is said in the same source:

But if his conduct is not flawless,
The world will look down on the bodhisattva.
This is like a fire covered with ashes,
Whereby sentient beings will be fried in hell.

This is taught in the context of protecting others from harm.

If a bodhisattva does not protect his body and speech from faulty behavior, others will lose faith. He will be looked down upon, and when others then proceed to the lower realms, he himself will be at fault. The same source states:

Therefore, it is taught
By the Victorious One in the *Supreme Jeweled Cloud Sutra*
That whatever creates distrust in sentient beings
Should carefully be relinquished.

Thus, it explains elaborately, quoting the sutras.

Moreover, Lord Atisha said:

Do not investigate the faults of others, but examine your own faults, and get rid of them like bad blood.

He also said:

One's own faults should be proclaimed.

Dromtonpa also spoke the following:

Pry into your own faults, then you will be wise.

Potowa explained:

Also, as an ordinary being, it is most important to give up your confusion for the benefit of sentient beings.

Kharagpa said:

Without conceiving of the faults of others,
Be aware of your own faults, and give them up.

Shabopa explained:

Without realizing my own faults, even though they are big, I realize the faults of others, even though they are tiny.

In such ways he would belittle himself.

Furthermore, from Gyalse Togme himself:

> While not possessing the slightest qualities of learnedness, right-eousness, and excellence, you proudly boast of yourself as excellent. You do not see your own faults, even though they are as huge as Mount Meru, but you see the faults of others, even though they are as tiny as dust motes.
>
> You keep the benefit for yourself in your heart but say that you are performing the benefit of others. Having disguised yourself as a Dharma practitioner, you accomplish only arrogance in this life. Never having examined your past behavior, you are fooling yourself.

In this way he disapproved of himself.

# GIVING UP PROCLAIMING THE
# FAULTS OF BODHISATTVAS

*If, due to negative emotions, one speaks of the faults of other bodhisattvas,*
*Oneself will become corrupted.*
*Hence, it is the practice of bodhisattvas not to speak of the faults of those*
*Who have entered the Great Vehicle.*

If an individual who has entered the Great Vehicle becomes influenced by
negative emotions in general, and jealousy in particular, and so judges the behavior of other bodhisattvas and then proclaims their faults, he himself will
become stained by downfalls and stray from the path of the Great Vehicle.
Hence, one must control one's speech and avoid speaking of even the tiniest
fault of another sentient being. In particular, one must refrain from speaking
of any faults of a person who, in terms of the Great and the Lesser Vehicles, has
entered the former. This is the practice whereby all bodhisattvas refrain from
examining others' faults and from speaking of them.

From *Purposeful Expressions*:

Do not investigate the faults of others,
And do not bother with what they have or have not done.

The *Compendium of Trainings* says, following the sutras:

Three times during day and night,
One bows one's head to all bodhisattvas.
Even if they always appear engaged in selfish pursuits,
Do not search for any mistake of theirs even in the slightest.

Hence, it is taught that it is not permissible to look for even the slightest
mistake in any sentient being, and in particular in those who have entered the

Great Vehicle. In the same way, it is said in the same source that after the Tathagata had perceived the actual empowerment, he said:

> An ordinary individual cannot comprehend the constitution of another individual. Only I and those who are similar to me comprehend the constitution of an individual.

And:

> Do not judge others saying that he is like this and she is like that.

Many such statements are made considering how to protect oneself from harm.

The *Seal Sutra of the Development of Faithful Strength* says the following:

> Compared to someone who imprisons all sentient beings out of anger, the one who has become upset with a bodhisattva and sits with his back turned against him, saying that he will not look at this awful one anymore, produces infinitely greater evil.

And:

> Compared to stealing the food of all the sentient beings of this world, to look down on any bodhisattva is of greater fault.

Likewise, in the *Seal Sutra That Regards Certainty and Uncertainty* and in the *Sutra of the Magical Ascertainment of Utter Peace* it is explained how the field of virtue and nonvirtue brought about in relation to bodhisattvas will be extremely powerful.

*The Way of the Bodhisattva* as well states:

> The one who harbors an evil thought
> Against a bodhisattva, such a lord of generosity,
> Will remain in hell for as many eons
> As there were moments of his meanness.

If one angrily says anything unpleasant or defamatory to a bodhisattva who has brought forth the mind of enlightenment, this will become a negative factor.

As for the antidote to this, it is the virtuous factors of bringing forth the notion that all bodhisattvas are one's teachers and of proclaiming their actual qualities in the ten directions.

In the *Sutra Requested by Kashyapa* it is said:

> I give rise to the notion that all sentient beings are my teachers. If
> you wonder why, it is because one cannot know whether someone's
> faculties have matured or not.

Hence, having given rise to the notion that all sentient beings are our teachers, it is important to train in pure perception.

Also, in *Letter to a Friend,* it is taught that just as there are four types of mango fruit, there are four types of humans. Especially when relating to those who have ripened on the inside but not yet on the outside, one is at the greatest risk of accumulating evil. This is similar to an unseen great abyss or a fire pit covered with ashes ,and one is therefore advised to be careful.

Furthermore, Lord Atisha has said:

> Do not look for the delusions of others
> But broadcast their qualities.

As well as:

> The individual who already possesses the eye of Dharma
> And the sentient being who is a mere beginner in the Dharma—
> You should have the notion of both being your teacher.
> When looking at sentient beings,
> See them as your parents or your children.

Dromtonpa also said:

> Leave others' faults alone; this then is virtue.

Potowa said the following:

> All sentient beings possess faults, so do not pay attention to nor
> think about any of their faults.

As well as:

> In general, accumulating evil in relation to somebody exceedingly
> excellent such as a bodhisattva will be the broom that sweeps away
> all one's virtue. In particular, this will fling bodhichitta far away.
> We can never be sure who is a bodhisattva and who is not.

And:

> Hence, do not examine the faults of any sentient being, and es-
> pecially do not look for faults in your master.

Kharagpa said:

> The outer behavior of that master
> Who teaches the Great Vehicle might not be beautiful,
> But since you do not know his inner realization,
> Do not conceive of faults in the master.

Langri Tangpa explained:

> An individual cannot grasp the capacity of another individual, so
> do not belittle anyone!

Chekawa said, "Do not point out anybody's handicap." And he continued,
"Just mind your own business!"

In this way they taught that it is not right to speak of the faults of others,
saying that someone has a deranged discipline and so forth. Moreover, it is in
general inappropriate to think about the faults of any sentient being, and in
particular to think of the faults of someone who has entered the door of Dharma.

Furthermore, Gyalse Togme himself said:

> In general, chatter is pointless. Nonvirtue increases, and in par-
> ticular, through despising others, one will be brought down and
> become stained by flaws. Attachment and aversion will increase
> and, in particular, the person and the Dharma will separate.
> Therefore, be terrified about despising others.

Moreover:

> When, due to jealousy, I despise the Dharma and the individual,
> My virtue decreases and others' minds become disturbed.
> Therefore, except when it is for the definite benefit of others,
> Do not express others' faults.

He himself practiced in this way.

## 33

# GIVING UP ATTACHMENT TO THE
# BENEFACTOR'S HOUSEHOLD

*As quarreling back and forth in order to gain honor and wealth*
*Degenerates the activities of learning, reflecting, and meditating,*
*It is the practice of bodhisattvas to give up all attachment*
*To the households of family, friends, and sponsors.*

Because of attachment to sponsors and friends who grant us honor and
possessions, those who have entered the Great Vehicle may, for the sake of
such honor and gain, argue back and forth with each other. This will cause a
degeneration of all the activities of the holy Dharma, such as learning, reflecting, and meditating. One must therefore give up attachment to the resi-
dences of sponsors and friends. This is the practice whereby all bodhisattvas
abandon attachment to those households that are sources of gain and honor.

From the *Sutra Inspiring Supreme Intention*:

> You should be watchful of gain and honor, since they produce at-
> tachment. You should also be watchful of gain and honor since
> they destroy mindfulness. In the same way, you should be watch-
> ful because they produce shamelessness and immodesty, make
> you regard the houses of friends as places for alms, make you
> miserly, and make you abandon friends and be unfriendly.

Moreover:

> In this way, a bodhisattva should examine all shortcomings of gain
> and honor. Having investigated them, he should decrease his de-
> sires and should not gather more.

And:

> Someone with few desires lacks all such shortcomings. For that
> one there are no hindrances for the teachings of the Buddha.

More:

> Having understood the benefits in this way, a learned bodhisattva
> should, in order to give up all honor and gain, abide sincerely and
> be content with few desires.

In this way, it teaches the faults of honor and gain and the benefits of fewer
desires and contentment.

The *Sutra Requested by Kashyapa* states:

> The bondage of view and the bondage of honor, gain, and fame
> Are the most severe types of bondage for all ordained ones;
> So it is taught by all the noble ones.
> Therefore, they must always be abandoned by the ordained.

*The Way of the Bodhisattva* says the following:

> "I have many possessions and am extremely revered,
> And many people are fond of me."
> If you are arrogant like this,
> After death expect the onset of your fears.

Moreover:

> People have had abundant possessions,
> Were famous, sweetly renowned;
> But where have they gone now,
> With all their baggage of fame and renown?

Furthermore, Lord Atisha said:

> Honor and gain are tight chains
> For all the ordained.
> One who frees himself from this bondage
> Is like a lotus within fire.[28]

Shabopa said the following:

> I cannot stand it if I see others becoming wealthy and famous.

In this way he disapproved of himself and explained how it is a great fault to praise yourself and put others down for the sake of honor and gain.

Nyugrumpa said:

> You should give rise to the notion of honor and gain being like a trap or a net.

Furthermore, from Gyalse Togme himself:

> Since honor and gain bind you, cut your fondness for sense pleasures.

As well as:

> Although you try laboriously
> To achieve all the perfections of this life, such as honor and gain,
> There is no certainty that you will accomplish them.
> Even if you achieve them, your craving will increase dramatically,
> Just like a tongue of fire increases when more firewood is added.

Moreover:

> Possessing a mind of contentment is the ultimate wealth.
> Being free from attachment to anything is the ultimate happiness.

He himself practiced accordingly.

34

GIVING UP UTTERING

HARSH WORDS

*Harsh words disturb the minds of others*
*And cause the bodhisattva's conduct to degenerate.*
*Therefore, it is the practice of bodhisattvas*
*To give up harsh words, which are unpleasant for others.*

Failing to examine the faults of one's speech, one may utter extremely harsh words and thereby disturb the minds of others. Moreover, in this way one falls away from excellent conduct, for when bodhisattvas speak, they must speak gently, in a balanced and pleasant way. Therefore, to utter harsh words is a great fault.

Hence, when speaking to others, to first examine and then to refrain from uttering any harsh words that will be unpleasant for the listener is the practice whereby all bodhisattvas give up unpleasant talk.

As the *Abhidharma Treasury* states:

Harsh words are those that are unpleasant.

Harsh words are those unpleasant words, which, when brought forth by any of the three poisons, become the basis for torment in the minds of those sentient beings toward whom they are directed.

Harsh words can be expressed in a number of ways. They may be true or false; they may concern someone's family, three doors, discipline, etc.; they may relate to hidden or obvious faults; or they may incite others to criticize in a way that will be understood by a particular third party.

If one expresses oneself in any way, gentle or harsh, with a motivation that is not entirely benevolent, the expression is to be classified as harsh words. In the scriptures that demonstrate the effects of karma, numerous shortcomings of harsh words are taught.

The *Compendium of Trainings* says, quoting the sutras:

> No bodhisattva should utter words that harm sentient beings. The same is the case with words that cause anguish or are unpleasant or painful. Having given up such mistaken ways of expression, one must always be gentle and without frivolousness.

Quoting in a similar way, it explains further that one must speak gently, softly, and delightfully.

Likewise, from *The Supreme Continuity*:

> That which comes first for a bodhisattva, with respect to benefiting all sentient beings, is pleasant talk.

From *The Way of the Bodhisattva*:

> When speaking, I should speak appropriately and the truth,
> With clear meaning and pleasantly;
> Not motivated out of desire and hatred should I speak,
> But gently and in moderation.

From *Letter to a Friend*:

> The Victorious One said that there is pleasant speech, true speech, and
>     false speech;
> The words of all sentient beings
> Are like honey, like flowers, and like excrement.
> Among these three ways of speaking, give up the last.

The Victorious One taught that sentient beings use three kinds of speech: speaking pleasantly in a way that the listener appreciates, speaking the truth, and speaking falsely. Those words are, respectively, the ones that make others happy and are like honey; the ones that are beautiful, praiseworthy, and like a flower; and the ones that are condemnable and like excrement. Among these three kinds, rely on the first two and give up the last. Thus, faulty speech is generally to be shunned.

Furthermore, from Lord Atisha:

> Those words that are unpleasant to the minds of others—
> A wise one throws them far away.

As well as:

> Always smiling and with a mind full of love, speak well and without anger.

Kharagpa said the following:

> Do not cast the poisonous arrow of harsh words.
> Give up anger, an evil state of mind.

Chekawa advised, "Never get caught in cycles of retaliation," and "Never strike at the heart."

One must not utter harsh words in return for the harsh words uttered by others. Moreover, do not speak crude words, such as curses and proclamations of people's hidden faults.

Moreover, from Gyalse Togme himself:

> Much talk may produce bad karma.

As well as:

> We cannot use a bad expression against anyone.

In addition, he would never call anyone simply by his name, but instead used respectful titles such as lama, teacher, master, geshe, chief, or lord. Even his servant, Dazang, he would call Teacher Dazang.

The four Dharmas—examining one's confusion, so that it may be dispelled, and so forth, which are the topics of this and the past three chapters, are to be found in the *Sutra Inspiring Supreme Intention*.

This sutra states the following:

> Maitreya, if a person of the Bodhisattva Vehicle is endowed with the four Dharmas, he will, at the time of the destruction of the Dharma in the last five hundred years, be free of harm and injury and become blissfully liberated. What are these four Dharmas? To analyze one's own confusion, not to expose the faults of other individuals of the Bodhisattva Vehicle, not to regard the residences of your friends, etc., as sources for alms, and to give up uttering unpleasant words.

# 35

## TRAINING IN GIVING UP

## NEGATIVE EMOTIONS

*When habituated to negative emotions, the antidotes can*
*    hardly reverse them.*
*Therefore, as soon as attachment and so forth arise,*
*It is the practice of bodhisattvas to, in the moment of mindfulness,*
*Take up the weaponlike antidote and destroy the negative emotions.*

When the various negative emotions of attachment and so forth arise, if
one lets them manifest without relying on an antidote, one becomes gradually habituated and accustomed to them. Then it will be very difficult to reverse
and abandon them in the future.

Therefore, a person who is mindful of what to accept and reject and is conscientious with respect to whatever happens with his three doors will apply
the antidote as an extremely sharp weapon. With this antidote, he crushes and
leaves behind the negative emotions, such as attachment, whenever they are
about to arise or as soon as they have arisen. This is the practice whereby all
bodhisattvas rely on the antidote against negative emotions.

From *Ornament of the Sutras:*

Negative emotions destroy oneself, they destroy sentient beings,
and they destroy discipline.

More from *The Way of the Bodhisattva:*

All enemies, such as craving, anger, and so forth,
Have neither arms nor legs
And are neither brave nor bright.
How then could I become incarcerated by them?

All negative emotions produce, in this life as well as in all future lives, unwholesomeness, suffering, and mental unhappiness. Causing harm to oneself and others, these faults are extremely great. Therefore, one needs to endeavor to abandon these negative emotions, which are so full of shortcomings.

From *The Way of the Bodhisattva:*

> My sole passion shall be now,
> Filled with bitterness, to meet negative emotions in battle.

As well as:

> Negative emotions, abandoned with the eye of knowledge,
> Where will you go now, when dispelled from my mind?

As for the manner of abandoning them, one places mindfulness as the watchman, who identifies them when they push their heads out. Perceiving them as the enemy, one must then stab them with the spear of the antidote. Otherwise, if we just accept them when they first appear, their strength will increase so that it will be difficult to give them up later.

The struggle with the enemy, the negative emotions, is very precisely taught in *The Way of the Bodhisattva*'s chapter entitled "Diligence." For instance:

> Just as an old warrior approaches
> The swords of an enemy on the battlefield,
> So shall I avoid the weapons of disturbing emotions
> And skillfully overcome these enemies.

So, just as a person accustomed to battles is skilled in fighting the enemy, we must be skilled in relying on the antidote against negative emotions.

> If someone drops the sword during battle,
> He will, out of fear, swiftly take it up again.
> Likewise, if we lose the weapon of mindfulness,
> We shall, terrified by the hells, retrieve it quickly.

If someone loses his sword while fighting with the enemy, he will immediately pick it up. In the same way, if we lose the weapon of the mindfulness of relying on the antidote, then out of fear of falling into the lower realms, we must immediately rely on mindfulness again.

> Just as poison transported on the current of blood
> Spreads throughout the whole body,

> Likewise, when negative emotions find an opportunity,
> Faults will flood my mind.

If we are wounded by a poisonous arrow, then we immediately need to cut open the wound and draw out the poison. In the same way, we need to put an end to negative emotions as soon as they arise.

> Be like a frightened man who is carrying a jar full of mustard oil
> While being threatened by a swordsman
> Who will kill him if he spills a single drop.
> This is how those who practice should discipline themselves.

When struggling with the enemy, the negative emotions, we must be extremely attentive and rely on mindfulness.

> Just as I would quickly leap up
> If a snake came into my lap,
> Likewise, if sleep and idleness overwhelm me,
> I will swiftly chase them away.

These quotes all demonstrate that we must reverse negative emotions as soon as they arise. Concerned that this might take up too much space, I did not elaborate in detail on the meaning of the examples.

Moreover, from Lord Atisha himself:

> When negative emotions appear, we need to remember the antidote. What need would there be of a Dharma that lets negative emotions run wild?

As well as:

> One who destroys negative emotions with an antidote as soon as
>     they arise—
> Such a supreme being is truly a hero.

And:

> We must crush all concepts as soon as they arise and let our antidotes strike fatally.

Dromtonpa also said:

> It is the Dharma if it becomes an antidote for negative emotions;
> If it does not become an antidote, it is not the Dharma.

Gonpawa said:

> In order to give up negative emotions, we need to know their shortcomings, their characteristics, their antidotes, and the causes for their arising. Having understood their shortcomings, one sees their faults and perceives them as one's enemies. If one does not understand their shortcomings, one will not realize that they are enemies. This reflection accords with *The Way of the Bodhisattva* and *Ornament of the Sutras*.

Moreover:

> In order to understand the characteristics of negative emotions, one studies the Abhidharma. At least one must study thecharacteristics of the five aggregates to understand the root and subsidiary disturbing emotions. When any emotion, such as attachment or aversion, arises, one then thinks, "This is that one. Now this one has come up!" This way of identifying them will combat the negative emotions.

Puchungwa spoke the following:

> Even when pressed down by the weight of negative emotions I will, clenching my teeth, never give up.

Potowa explained:

> Always being mindful, one needs to endeavor in examining one's own mindstream. One must relinquish and protect oneself from any negative emotion.

Ben Kungyal said the following:

> From now on I have nothing to do but wait continuously at the entrance gate to the castle of my mind with the spearlike antidote in hand. When the spear is raised, I am alert. If the spear is lowered, it means that I have become too loose.

Langri Tangpa said:

> Throughout daily activities one continuously examines one's being,
> And as soon as negative emotions arise,
> Since they are vicious to oneself and others,
> One must avert them directly with sudden force.

And:

> If you go somewhere else, or simply turn your face away, negative emotions may thereby also calm down.

Nyugrumpa:

> If negative emotions appear, by no means be lazy but reverse them with an antidote. If you are not able to reverse them, get up and prepare a mandala offering. Offer this to the lamas and the yidams and supplicate them. As you focus on them, recite wrathful mantras. Negative emotions will thereby calm down.

Moreover, from Gyalse Togme himself:

> Training in taming the thoughts of the three poisons during the post-meditation stage
> Is indispensable until all thoughts and appearances have arisen as dharmakaya.
> Hence, remember it when necessary.
> Do not let confused thoughts run wild, you *mani* reciters.

As well as:

> First, one must identify negative emotions upon arising;
> Then one must give them up having developed the strength of the antidote;
> And in the end, one should endeavor so that they do not reappear in the future.

He himself practiced in this way.

36

# TRAINING IN ACCOMPLISHING
# THE BENEFIT OF OTHERS
# THROUGH MINDFULNESS

*In short, whatever I may do throughout my activities,*
*I ask, "What is my mind doing?"*
*Thus, it is the practice of bodhisattvas to accomplish the benefit of others*
*With continuous mindfulness and conscientiousness.*

What is the condensed key point of all those stages of the bodhisattva practices that have been explained above? It is not to let mindfulness and conscientiousness degenerate. Whenever one engages in any of the four activities,
one must continuously keep watch by means of asking: "How is my mind doing? Is it virtuous or nonvirtuous?"

In this way, to accomplish the benefit of sentient beings with an excellent
supreme altruistic attitude is the fundamental and most precious key point of
all practices whereby bodhisattvas accomplish the two benefits.

*The Way of the Bodhisattva* says:

Those who wish to observe the trainings
Should guard their minds tightly.

In order to observe the trainings, one needs to guard the mind. If one won-
ders about how to guard one's mind, the same source says:

All those who wish to guard their mind
Must observe the mind persistently,
With mindfulness and conscientiousness.
Thus, I beseech you with folded hands.

Thus, it is taught that it is very important to always rely on mindfulness
in order to guard one's mind. Mindfulness means not forgetting any points
regarding what to accept and reject. This is extremely important, as it is explained in *Letter to a Friend*:

Carefully and truly observe mindfulness,
Because when it degenerates, all Dharmas are destroyed.

From *The Way of the Bodhisattva*:

If I tie the elephantlike mind tightly
With the rope of thorough mindfulness,
All fears will fade away.

These quotations demonstrate the benefits and faults of keeping mindfulness or letting it degenerate.

As for conscientiousness, it is to be aware of all activities of the three doors and to identify whether one's conduct is good or bad.

Concerning this, *The Way of the Bodhisattva* says:

To examine again and again
The constitution of body and mind—
This, in short, is precisely
The characteristic of being conscientious.

It is taught that whether one practices sutra or mantra, all the practices depend on conscientiousness and mindfulness. It is therefore indeed very important.

Likewise, from a sutra:

All that may be called virtuous qualities
Have carefulness as their root.

As to the essence of carefulness, this root of virtuous qualities, it is to abandon nonvirtuous deeds and to engage in virtuous deeds instead. There are many faults and benefits of carelessness and carefulness, but in this context, this is how they are described.

In short, bodhisattvas train during all their activities by being endowed with mindfulness and carefulness, as it is taught in the *Sutra of Completely Pure Conduct*. Embracing whatever they do with the altruistic attitude, they must train in letting everything, either directly or indirectly, become the cause for the benefit of others and for enlightenment.

It is taught in the *Sutra of Instructions to the King* that if the mind of aspiration that strives for complete enlightenment for the benefit of others does not degenerate, all the trainings of the bodhisattvas are contained therein.

The *Compendium of Trainings* also says:

> Throughout all activities, one must train in the mind of enlightenment, and let all be preceded by the mind of enlightenment.

Moreover:

> The training of a bodhisattva is nothing but this—to fully purify your mind.

If one gives up the mind that wishes to attain enlightenment for the benefit of others, both the bodhichitta of aspiration and the bodhichitta of action will have been abandoned. Therefore, even at present, regardless of whether one is able to benefit others directly or not, one must, by no means, let the intention to benefit others degenerate.

From *Commentary on the Enlightened Mind*:

> Even though you might not yet have the power to benefit others,
> Always engender the intention to benefit.
> Whoever possesses that intention
> Is in fact already active.

Moreover, Lord Atisha said:

> With mindfulness, conscientiousness, and carefulness,
> Always protect the sense doors.
> Day and night and throughout the three times,
> Examine your mindstream repeatedly.

He continues:

> The supreme quality is the great benevolent intention;
> The supreme oral instruction is to always watch one's own mind;
> The supreme friends are mindfulness and conscientiousness.

Gonpawa said the following:

> Besides watching one's own mind day and night, what else is there to do?

Potowa explained:

> Through being mindful and conscientious during the four activities, one will, while walking, walk with loving-kindness and the mind of enlightenment. While moving around, one will move

with loving-kindness and the mind of enlightenment. Likewise, while engaging in any activity of the three doors, such as sleeping, eating, and so forth, one should always act and train by means of loving-kindness and the mind of enlightenment.

Langri Tangpa said:

Since in the Great Vehicle there is nothing else to do except benefit sentient beings, your armor of altruism should not be weak.

Sharawa also said:

At all times you should embrace your activities with mindfulness and conscientiousness. Whatever action you are about to undertake with your body, speech, and mind, let it be prepared by the mind of enlightenment.

According to the *Sutra of the Pure Field of Engagement*, it is taught that whatever action one does, one should cultivate the intention to benefit others. Geshe Dragyabpa explained:

At all times, you must again and again be mindful, survey your mind conscientiously, and be permeated by carefulness.

Furthermore, Gyalse Togme himself explained:

By being endowed with mindfulness and carefulness, your mind will always be gentle.

And:

In short, through mindfulness one examines well one's being
So that what is taught in the Dharma
And one's own way of practicing are not in conflict.
It is extremely important to gain such self-determination.

He continued:

Since it is the speciality of the Great Vehicle, develop the intent to be of benefit to beings.
Since it is the conduct of the bodhisattvas, let your three doors accomplish the benefit of others.

He himself practiced in this way.

37

# DEDICATION OF VIRTUE
# TOWARD COMPLETE
# ENLIGHTENMENT

*In order that all the virtue accomplished diligently in this way*
*May clear away the suffering of limitless beings,*
*It is the practice of bodhisattvas to dedicate all virtue toward enlightenment,*
*With the knowledge of the three spheres' complete purity.*

Virtue results from training in and accomplishing persistently the practices of the bodhisattvas as explained above with a great diligence that makes one joyfully enter into one's practice. As exemplified by that virtue, all virtuous deeds accumulated in the three times by oneself and all others must without exception be dedicated so that they may dispel all the suffering of the limitless gatherings of beings and become the cause of perfect enlightenment for the welfare of others. One does so with the knowledge that realizes the absence of truth and that is totally free from the stains of apprehending a true existence of the three spheres, i.e., the object of dedication, the one who dedicates, and the process of dedication. This is the practice whereby all bodhisattvas skillfully avoid any dissipation of the virtuous accumulations and instead make them increase further and further.

From a sutra:

Everything is circumstantial
And depends entirely on one's aspiration.
The one who makes an aspiration
Will achieve its result accordingly.

Thus, since the one who dedicates any accumulated root of virtue achieves the result accordingly, it is necessary to dedicate one's virtue.

Concerning this, it is said in *The Way of the Bodhisattva*:

> Whether actually or indirectly,
> One persists in nothing but the benefit of sentient beings
> And must dedicate everything toward enlightenment
> For the sole benefit of sentient beings.

Hence, one must dedicate in order to attain perfect enlightenment for the benefit of sentient beings. This is the supreme dedication, since by dedicating in this way, the root of virtue will not become exhausted before reaching enlightenment but will only further increase.

The *Sutra Requested by Inexhaustible Intelligence* says the following:

> When dedicated toward enlightenment, the root of virtue will not become exhausted before the attainment of the essence of enlightenment.

On the other hand, the effect will not be utterly inexhaustible if one fails to dedicate, dedicates wrongly, dedicates the virtue as cause for inferior cyclic existence, or dedicates it as cause for mere liberation. But if one dedicates the root of virtue toward perfect enlightenment, it will become inexhaustible.

One sutra uses a drop of water that falls on dry ground as an example of a lack of dedication and so forth, while a drop of water that falls into the ocean exemplifies a dedication toward supreme enlightenment.

*The Way of the Bodhisattva* uses the analogy of the fruit of the miraculous tree and the plantain tree.[29] Concerning the manner of dedication, it is said in a sutra:

> If done with attributes, it is not dedication;
> If free of attributes, it is the enlightened dedication.

Hence, a dedication made with the belief in the true existence of the three spheres of observations—the object of dedication, the one who dedicates, and the act of dedication—is not a completely pure dedication.

Aside from being mere convention and mental imputation, the three spheres do not truly exist in their own right. To dedicate with such an insight is the dedication of complete purity.

Moreover, Lord Atisha said:

> Even though one may endeavor in virtue with the three doors day and night, if one does not know the dedication toward perfect enlightenment, it can become exhausted by a few wrong thoughts.

Also:

> You should endeavor in all virtues in various ways and then im-
> mediately dedicate such virtue toward omniscience. If you do that,
> even an accumulation of merit will turn into wisdom, and like-
> wise, the accumulation of wisdom will become meritorious.

Moreover:

> Whatever virtue is accumulated throughout the three times,
> Dedicate it toward unsurpassable great enlightenment.
> The merit will rub off on sentient beings.

Dromtonpa said:

> While seeing all phenomena without conceptualizing the three
> spheres, the root of virtue is to be dedicated toward all sentient
> beings and universal complete enlightenment.

Potowa:

> All roots of virtue are controlled by aspirations. Therefore, it is
> taught that after accumulating any virtue it is important to make
> prayers of aspiration.

Kharagpa explained:

> Even if the quantity of virtue is tiny,
> The results may increase inexhaustibly.
> Before all dedication of the three times,
> Give rise to the mind of enlightenment.

Geshe Dragyabpa said the following:

> It should be so that one has nothing to do aside from persevering
> as much as one can in whatever Dharma practice one may know,
> as well as making aspiration prayers and so forth for the welfare of
> all sentient beings.

Sharawa taught that the vast skillful method is to practice all virtues, such
as the six paramitas, with the wish to attain buddhahood for the welfare of all
beings. Moreover, the skillful method of complete purity is to embrace this
with the insight that realizes the lack of truth. The inexhaustible skillful method
is to dedicate the virtues toward unsurpassable enlightenment so that they will
not become exhausted before the attainment of the core of enlightenment.

In addition, Gyalse Togme said:

> To dedicate any merit accumulated, whether small or great,
> With the purity of the three spheres
> So that all beings without limit may attain enlightenment
> Is the supreme method for merit to become boundless.

He himself, when having done anything virtuous, offered vast and powerful dedications such as this one:

> Just as the bodhisattvas Manjushri and Samantabhadra
> Have dedicated their virtue,
> I dedicate this virtue to the practice of the highest good
> With this supreme dedication praised by the buddhas of all times.

PART 3

# THE CONDENSED MEANING
# OF THE CONCLUSION

# THE CONDENSED MEANING
# OF THE CONCLUSION

THE CONCLUSION is divided into five topics:
1. The reasons for composing
2. Demonstrating the practices to be free of confusion
3. Humbling pride and requesting forgiveness
4. Dedicating the virtue of composing the treatise toward enlightenment
5. Colophon endowed with the four excellences

## THE REASONS FOR COMPOSING

> *The meaning taught in the sutras, tantras, and treatises,*
> *I have, following the teachings of the sacred ones,*
> *Formulated as these "Thirty-Seven Practices of the Bodhisattvas"*
> *For the sake of those who wish to train on the path of the bodhisattvas.*

That is to say, I have extracted the meaning that was excellently taught in the Victorious One's sutras and tantras, the *Bodhisattva Pitaka*, and so forth, as well as in the commentaries on their enlightened intent. Following the explanations of all the sacred forefathers in general, I have relied in particular on Lord Atisha and his heirs, the spiritual teachers of the Kadam tradition, and on my own spiritual teachers.

In this way, condensing all into thirty-seven practices whereby one may genuinely train in all the disciplines of the bodhisattvas, I have composed this text for the sake of all those fortunate ones who wish to train on the path of the bodhisattvas.

## DEMONSTRATING THE PRACTICES
## TO BE FREE OF CONFUSION

> *Because I am of inferior intelligence and have little learning,*
> *This is not a composition that will delight the scholars;*

*But because it relies on the teachings of the sutras and the sacred ones,*
*I believe the "Practices of the Bodhisattvas" is free from mistakes.*

That is to say, I, the composer, was born with an inferior intelligence, and my knowledge derived from training is ephemeral. Therefore, with respect to literary style, my words lack all excellence, which otherwise would delight the hearts of the learned ones who possess eminent intellect and are great scholars of the scriptures.

However, in terms of what has been expressed, it is not my personal creation. This is, as was explained before, based on the sutras and the teachings of the sacred ones and in this way is an excellent composition. Therefore, I believe that these practices or trainings of the bodhisattvas are free of any delusion or mistake.

## HUMBLING PRIDE AND REQUESTING FORGIVENESS

*However, since the vast conduct of the bodhisattvas*
*Is difficult to comprehend by one of inferior intellect such as me,*
*I ask all the sacred ones for forgiveness*
*For a multitude of faults, including contradictions and incoherence.*

As was just explained, I do indeed believe that these explanations of the practices of bodhisattvas are free of delusion. However, since the ways of conduct of all bodhisattvas are limitless, splendid, profound, and vast like the ocean, they are, for someone like me who is of inferior intellect, difficult to comprehend.

Therefore, I ask the genuinely trustworthy ones for forgiveness for whatever multitude of faults there might be, such as contradictions between earlier and later statements and any incoherence between the meaning and the words I have used in my explanations.

## DEDICATING THE VIRTUE OF COMPOSING TOWARD ENLIGHTENMENT

*By the virtue resulting from this, may all beings,*
*Through the relative and ultimate supreme mind of enlightenment,*
*Become equal to the protector Avalokiteshvara,*
*Remaining in neither extreme of existence or peace.*

Through the virtue resulting from explaining the trainings of the bodhisattvas, may the knowledge that directly realizes ultimate emptiness—the
ultimate mind of enlightenment—arise in the minds of all beings.

Moreover, may an intention that strives for perfect enlightenment for the
benefit of beings, led by great compassion—the relative mind of enlightenment—spring forth.

Having thus swiftly brought forth these two aspects of mind, may all beings, through supreme knowledge, not abide in the extreme of samsara, and
through the strength of compassion and the Great Vehicle's mind of enlightenment, may they also not abide in the extreme of peace.

May they hence become equal to the protector of the three worlds, the
supreme, incomparable Avalokiteshvara, who, having actualized perfect enlightenment, does not abide in the two extremes. Instead, for as long as existence remains, he benefits sentient beings by means of nonreferential great
compassion and the eminent activity of skillful means.

## THE COLOPHON ENDOWED
## WITH FOUR EXCELLENCES

The author's colophon reads:

> *This was composed in the Ngulchu Rinchen cave by the monk Tögme, a pro-
> ponent of scripture and reasoning, for the purpose of benefiting myself and
> others.*

This forms a colophon endowed with the four excellences in terms of content, purpose, author, and location.

## COMMENTATOR'S COLOPHON

As for this commentary on the practices of the bodhisattvas, *The Unity of Scripture
and Oral Instructions*, I have used as a foundation texts such as the condensed version of the life story of the precious Gyalse, which was composed by Nyenpo
Palrin and is considered to be the meaning commentary on *The Thirty-Seven
Practices*. On several occasions, I have mentioned how Gyalse Tögme himself
practiced; the details of this may be learned from that life story.

Moreover, for the initial and concluding parts of the text I have given only
a literal commentary on the verses. Throughout the main part, for each point
of the thirty-seven practices I have first given a concise literal commentary,
and subsequently, in the customary way of explaining a scripture, I have brought

in a few quotations from scriptures such as the sutras. These have then been ornamented by various advice from Lord Atisha and the masters of his lineage, as well as with the nectarlike speech, manifest in the form of oral instructions, of the precious bodhisattva Gyalse Togme himself.

Although I have thus treated scriptures and oral instructions in different sections, these are not in contradiction.

Moreover, if one were to explain this scripture elaborately, the text would become extremely lengthy, and I do not believe such would serve any purpose either. Therefore, I have brought only a few citations, often by stating merely the first verse of a stanza, and have generally kept the explanations brief.

Furthermore, if one is interested in an even more condensed version, one could, as one wished, simply read the literal commentary on the root verses, possibly with the addition of a few of the scriptural explanations.

The reason for chiefly relying on the instructions of the Kadam masters is that most of Gyalse Togme's teachings, including the present one, precisely follow the Kadam way in terms of mind training and so forth. Moreover, the one who requested that I write this commentary has himself great interest in the Kadam style of mind training. In general, there is nothing particularly beneficial in bringing one quotation after another, yet here I have progressively quoted the sacred ones whose words contain powerful blessings so that I and those of equal fortune may be repeatedly inspired toward faith and renunciation and may experience certainty.

> The explanations of the scripture, an excellent vase adorned with
>     jewels
> And filled with the nectar of oral instructions,
> Bestow upon all the gatherings of fortunate beings wishing for
>     liberation
> The glory of supreme immortal peace.

> By the wholesome deeds that have come about because of these efforts,
> May all beings enter the door of the Supreme Vehicle,
> Fully mature in the conduct of the bodhisattvas,
> And become rich with the glory of an ocean of excellent qualities.

> Whatever harm I have caused to sentient beings either in thought
>     or deed
> When wandering deluded so long in existence,

May all that which has caused anguish in the hearts of the victorious
  ones and their children
Become entirely cleansed and purified.

From today forward, may our efforts in body, speech, and mind
Never become the cause for harming others,
But may they always, for all limitless sentient beings,
Solely be the cause of benefit and happiness.

When vicious beings answer good with bad,
And when the mean and low ones mock us and so forth,
May we, to all those who do great harm and are difficult to tolerate,
In reply to their harm work only to accomplish their welfare.

Thus, may all beings not yet tamed by the victorious ones
Be established at the level of the victorious ones;
May we become the carriers of the victorious ones' activity
And so accomplish all their deeds.

Having passed through the inconceivable gates
Of the victorious ones' skilled conduct,
May we, by actualizing the illusionlike liberations,
Swiftly accomplish the qualities of perfection, ripening, and
  purification.

Further, may the doctrine and its upholders increase and develop,
And may I and all beings become happy and joyful,
Temporarily achieving the higher realms, and ultimately achieving
  supreme liberation.
May the benefit for myself and others be effortlessly and
  spontaneously accomplished.

Repeatedly exhorted by the sacred lord of refuge Orgyen Lhundrub, a master and lord of yogins who lives as a monk at the monastery of Ser Lhatse, this was composed by Chökyi Dragpa.

May it be virtuous.
Virtue! Virtue! Virtue!

# THE THIRTY-SEVEN PRACTICES OF
# A BODHISATTVA

## BY GYALSE TOGME

Namo Lokeshvaraya

*Seeing that all phenomena are beyond coming or going,*
*He strives solely for the benefit of sentient beings.*
*To the supreme master and protector, Avalokiteshvara,*
*I prostrate continuously and respectfully with body, speech, and mind.*

*The perfectly enlightened ones, sources of benefit and happiness,*
*Appear from having accomplished the holy Dharma.*
*Since that accomplishment depends on knowing the practices,*
*I will here explain the practice of the bodhisattvas.*

*At this time of having obtained the rare great ship of freedoms and riches,*
*Without any distraction day and night,*
*In order to liberate oneself and others from the ocean of samsara*
*Is the practice of the bodhisattvas.*

*Toward friends, attachment rages like a river;*
*Toward enemies, hatred blazes like fire.*
*Therefore, it is the practice of bodhisattvas to give up that home,*
*Where the darkness of stupidity, of forgetting what to accept and reject, prevails.*

*Abandoning negative places, disturbing emotions gradually subside;*
*Being free from distraction, the practice of virtue spontaneously increases;*
*With brightened awareness one feels confidence in the Dharma;*
*To adhere to solitude is the practice of the bodhisattvas.*

*Separated from each and every long-acquainted companion,*
*Leaving behind hard-earned wealth and possessions,*

*Guest-like consciousness abandons its guesthouse, the body;*
*To give up concern for this life is the practice of the bodhisattvas.*

*If, while befriending someone, the three poisons increase,*
*The activities of study, reflection, and meditation degenerate,*
*And love and compassion disappear,*
*Then it is the practice of the bodhisattvas to give up this bad company.*

*When relying on the sacred spiritual friend, our faults become exhausted*
*And our good qualities increase like the waxing moon.*
*It is the practice of bodhisattvas to value such a sacred spiritual friend*
*As more precious than their own body.*

*Bound, themselves, in the prison of samsara,*
*Whom are the worldly gods able to protect?*
*Therefore, it is the practice of the bodhisattvas*
*To go for refuge in the three unfailing Jewels.*

*All the sufferings of the lower realms, so extremely difficult to bear,*
*Are taught by the Sage to be the fruit of one's evil actions.*
*Therefore, it is the practice of bodhisattvas*
*To constantly refrain from evil actions, even at the cost of one's life.*

*The happiness of the three realms is like a dewdrop on the tip of a blade of grass;*
*It perishes by itself from one instant to the next.*
*Hence, it is the practice of a bodhisattva*
*To strive for the supreme level of liberation, always unchanging.*

*When all our mothers, who have cherished us since beginningless time, are suffering,*
*Of what use then is our own happiness?*
*Therefore, it is the practice of bodhisattvas to engender the mind of enlightenment*
*For the sake of liberating sentient beings beyond limit.*

*All suffering, without exception, springs from the desire for one's own happiness;*
*Perfect enlightenment is born from a mind intent on benefiting others.*
*Therefore, it is the practice of bodhisattvas*
*To authentically exchange one's own happiness for the sufferings of others.*

*If someone, swayed by great desire,*
*Steals all one's wealth or incites others to do so,*

*It is the practice of bodhisattvas to dedicate to that person*
*One's physical body, enjoyments, and virtues of the three times.*

*Even if someone were to cut off one's head,*
*Though one is free from the slightest fault,*
*It is the practice of bodhisattvas to take all wrongdoing upon oneself*
*Through the force of compassion.*

*Even if someone proclaims all kinds of defamation about me*
*Throughout the three-thousand-fold universe,*
*It is the practice of bodhisattvas*
*To praise that person's qualities repeatedly with a loving attitude.*

*Even if someone, amid a crowd of many people,*
*Reveals one's faults and utters harsh words,*
*It is the practice of the bodhisattvas to bow to that one respectfully*
*With the notion that this is one's spiritual teacher.*

*Even if someone for whom I have cared for as dearly as my own child*
*Perceives me as an enemy,*
*It is the practice of bodhisattvas to love this one devotedly,*
*Just as a mother loves her child stricken by disease.*

*Even if a person equal to or inferior to myself*
*Defames me due to the force of pride,*
*It is the practice of the bodhisattvas to venerate this one*
*Like the master upon the crown of my head.*

*Even if I am deprived of a livelihood, constantly belittled by everyone,*
*And stricken by a severe illness or demonic influence,*
*It is the practice of bodhisattvas to take upon oneself*
*All the suffering and evil of all beings without becoming depressed.*

*Though I may be eminently acclaimed, be revered by many beings,*
*And possess a fortune resembling Vaishravana's,*
*It is the practice of the bodhisattvas to remain without arrogance,*
*Having seen how the glory and riches of this existence are pointless.*

*If I do not tame the enemy that is my own anger,*
*Subduing outer enemies will only increase them.*

*Therefore, it is the practice of bodhisattvas to tame one's own being*
*By means of the armies of loving-kindness and compassion.*

*Sense pleasures are like salty water;*
*However much one partakes of them, craving will only increase.*
*Hence, it is the practice of bodhisattvas to abandon immediately*
*All objects that generate attachment.*

*Whatever appears is all one's own mind;*
*Mind itself is primordially beyond all mental constructs.*
*Knowing this, it is the practice of the bodhisattvas*
*Not to hold on to any attributes of perceiver and perceived.*

*When encountering a beautiful object,*
*One should consider it to be like a rainbow in summertime:*
*It appears attractive yet is not thought to be truly existent.*
*To so give up attachment is the practice of the bodhisattvas.*

*The various sufferings are just like the death of one's child in a dream;*
*How very tiring to grasp illusory appearances as being real!*
*Therefore, when encountering adverse circumstances,*
*It is the practice of bodhisattvas to regard them as illusions.*

*If, when wishing for enlightenment, one must give up even one's body,*
*So giving up external objects goes without question!*
*Therefore, it is the practice of the bodhisattvas to be generous*
*Without any hope for reward or positive result.*

*Lacking discipline, one will not accomplish one's own benefit,*
*And so the wish to accomplish the benefit of others will be laughable.*
*Therefore, it is the practice of the bodhisattvas to observe discipline*
*Free of any mundane ambitions.*

*For a bodhisattva who wishes for the enjoyments of virtue,*
*All harm-doers are like precious treasures.*
*Therefore, it is the practice of bodhisattvas to cultivate patience,*
*Free of hatred and animosity toward anyone.*

*Even the shravakas and pratyekabuddhas, who accomplish only their own benefit,*
*Are seen to be as persistent as those extinguishing a fire burning in their hair.*
*It is the practice of the bodhisattvas to muster diligence,*
*The source of all qualities, for the benefit of all beings.*

*Having understood that clear seeing, fully endowed with peaceful resting,*
*Completely destroys negative emotions,*
*It is the practice of bodhisattvas to cultivate a meditative concentration*
*That truly transcends the four formless realms.*

*Lacking knowledge, the five other paramitas are not sufficient*
*For the attainment of perfect enlightenment;*
*Hence, it is the practice of bodhisattvas to train in knowledge*
*Endowed with method and beyond conceptions of the three spheres.*

*When not examining one's own confusion,*
*It is possible to have the appearance of a Dharma practitioner while doing*
    *what is not Dharma.*
*Therefore, it is the practice of bodhisattvas to relinquish*
*Their own confusion, through continuously examining it.*

*If, due to negative emotions, one speaks of the faults of other bodhisattvas,*
*Oneself will become corrupted.*
*Hence, it is the practice of bodhisattvas not to speak of the faults of those*
*Who have entered the Great Vehicle.*

*As quarreling back and forth in order to gain honor and wealth*
*Degenerates the activities of learning, reflecting, and meditating,*
*It is the practice of bodhisattvas to give up all attachment*
*To the households of family, friends, and sponsors.*

*Harsh words disturb the minds of others*
*And cause the bodhisattva's conduct to degenerate.*
*Therefore, it is the practice of bodhisattvas*
*To give up harsh words, which are unpleasant for others.*

*When habituated to negative emotions, the antidotes can hardly reverse them.*
*Therefore, as soon as attachment and so forth arise,*

*It is the practice of bodhisattvas to, in the moment of mindfulness,*
*Take up the weaponlike antidote and destroy the negative emotions.*

*In short, whatever I may do throughout my activities,*
*I ask, "What is my mind doing?"*
*Thus, it is the practice of bodhisattvas to accomplish the benefit of others*
*With continuous mindfulness and conscientiousness.*

*In order that all the virtue accomplished diligently in this way*
*May clear away the suffering of limitless beings,*
*It is the practice of bodhisattvas to dedicate all virtue toward enlightenment,*
*With the knowledge of the three spheres' complete purity.*

*The meaning taught in the sutras, tantras, and treatises,*
*I have, following the teachings of the sacred ones,*
*Formulated as these "Thirty-Seven Practices of the Bodhisattvas"*
*For the sake of those who wish to train on the path of the bodhisattvas..*

*Because I am of inferior intelligence and have little learning,*
*This is not a composition that will delight the scholars;*
*But because it relies on the teachings of the sutras and the sacred ones,*
*I believe the "Practices of the Bodhisattvas" is free from mistakes.*

*However, since the vast conduct of the bodhisattvas*
*Is difficult to comprehend by one of inferior intellect such as me,*
*I ask all the sacred ones for forgiveness*
*For a multitude of faults, including contradictions and incoherence.*

*By the virtue resulting from this, may all beings,*
*Through the relative and ultimate supreme mind of enlightenment,*
*Become equal to the protector Avalokiteshvara,*
*Remaining in neither extreme, of existence or peace.*

*This was composed in the Ngulchu Rinchen cave by the monk Togme, a pro-*
*ponent of scripture and reasoning, for the purpose of benefiting myself and*
*others.*

# NOTES

1. Gyalse Togme is also known by the name Togme Zangpo (Thog med bzang po).
2. The translation of the commentary is based on the edition found in *Rgyal sras lag len rtsa 'grel* of *Si khron mi rigs dpe skrun khang*, 1992.
3. See E. Gene Smith, *Among Tibetan Texts: History and Literature of the Himalayan Plateau* (Boston: Wisdom Publications, 2002), pp. 235–50.
4. Tubten Chökyi Dragpa's Madhyamaka scholarship is available to the English reader in *Wisdom: Two Buddhist Commentaries on the Ninth Chapter of Shantideva's Bodhicharyavatara* (Peyzac-le-Moustier, France: Editions Padmakara, 1993).
5. Kelsang Chökyi Gyaltsen's (Skal bzang chos kyi rgyal mtshan) *History of Buddhism in Tibet and Mongolia* (*Bod sog chos 'byung* in *Gangs can rig brgya'i sgo 'byed lde mig*, vol. 18, 1993, p. 436) explains the origin of the Kadam school in the following way: "The great Lord, glorious Atisha, was the initiator, and the precious teacher [Dromtonpa] was the founder. While the three brothers [Potowa, Chen-ngawa, and Puchungwa] had made [the movement] spread and flourish, Langri Tangpa, Sharawa, and others caused it to expand even further."
6. These historical notes are primarily based on Michael Sweet's excellent article "Mental Purification *(Blo sbyong)*: A Native Tibetan Genre of Religious Literature" in *Tibetan Literature* by Cabezón and Jackson (New York: Snow Lion Publications, 1996) pp. 244–60, and in the "Historical and Thematic Introduction" by Michael J. Sweet and Leonard Zwilling in Geshe Lhundub Sopa's *Peacock in the Poison Grove* (Boston: Wisdom Publications, 2001), pp. 1–23.
7. In Kelsang Chökyi Gyaltsen's *Bod sog chos 'byung* (in *Gangs can rig brgya'i sgo 'byed lde mig*, vol. 18, 1993, pp. 460–61) it is mentioned how Atisha's activity had an influence on the emergence of the Kagyu, Sakya, and Gelug lineages. For instance, it is taught that the great translator Marpa (1012–97) met Atisha and received teachings from him. The outstanding master Gampopa (1097–1153) was a student of a direct disciple of Atisha and became known for joining the two spiritual rivers of Mahamudra and Kadampa. Gampopa's prolific disciple Pagmo Drupa (1110–70) received teachings from Geshe Dolpa (1059–1131), whom we often see quoted in this commentary. Moreover, Karmapa Dusum Khyenpa (1110–93) is said to have had instructions from a student of Sharawa (1070–1141) known as Naljorpa Sherab Dorje (eleventh century). As for the Sakya tradition, Panchen Sakya Jamyang (twelfth century) was a student of a disciple of Neuzurpa (1042–1118), and the famed Gelug forefather Tsongkhapa (1357–1419) received teachings from the Kadampas Khenchen Namkha Gyaltsen (fourteenth century) and Dragor Khenchen Chökhyab Zangpo (fourteenth century).
8. On the etymology of the term *blo sbyong*, see *Tibetan Literature*, pp. 245–46 and *Peacock in the Poison Grove*, pp. 15–17 (see n. 7 above).

9. *('ja' lus).* When a practitioner who has gained deep realization through the practice of the Great Perfection passes away, the five elements that form the physical body dissolve back into their essences, i.e., five-colored rainbow light.

10. In the *Bka' gdams chos 'byung (mtsho sngon mi rigs dpe skrun khang,* 1996) by Sonam Dragpa Gyaltsen (Bsod nams grags pa rgyal mtshan) it is said: "The spiritual friend, Dromtonpa, plus Naljorpa, Gonpawa, the three brothers, Neuzurpa, and Sharawa are renowned as the eight faces of the Kadampas."

11. Skt. *Abhidharmasamuccaya;* Tib. *Mngon pa kun btus.*

12. zang zing med pa'i sdug bsngal.

13. This story is told in Kelsang Chökyi Gyaltsen's *Bod sog chos 'byung* (in *Gangs can rig brgya'i sgo 'byed lde mig,* vol. 18, 1993, p. 467).

14. Kelsang Chökyi Gyaltsen in *Ldeb bco brgyad pa (Gangs can rig brgya'i sgo 'byed lde mig,* 1993, p. 436) explains that "'Kadam' implies the dawning of the words of the Buddha as oral instruction."

15. The other five texts are: *Compendium of Trainings (Śikṣāsamuccaya)* by Shantideva; *The Stages of a Bodhisattva (Bodhisattvabhūmi)* and the *Ornament of the Sutras (Mahāyānasūtrālaṃkāra)* by Maitreya via Asanga; *Garland of Buddha's Birth Stories (Jātakamālā)* by Aryashura; and *Purposeful Expressions (Udānavarga)* by Dharmatratta.

16. In order to understand the preciousness of human life, examples are taken from the scripture: for instance that of the blind turtle chancing to poke its head through a wooden yoke that is floating on the surface of the world ocean. Enumeration implies considering the way in which the inhabitants of the lower realms of existence are successively far more numerous than the inhabitants of the higher realms. Cause implies the contemplation on the way that vast accumulations of virtue based on pure discipline and directed by genuine aspiration are required for the achievement of a precious human body.

17. This quotation is from Chandrakirti's *Entering into the Middle Way.*

18. For instance objects that might have been stolen and so in fact belong to someone else.

19. The three kinds of training are discipline, meditation, and knowledge.

20. In the same way, to give up concern for this life is the best practice for all Dharma practitioners.

21. The central teaching of the *Sutra of the Wise and the Fool* is that of karma—cause and effect.

22. Here, the numbers are not specific but are used in an idiomatic sense.

23. This practice is known as *tonglen* in Tibetan. While breathing in, one mentally takes in all the misery and negativity of all sentient beings; while breathing out, one gives away all one's happiness and virtue to sentient beings.

24. Vaishravana is a god of wealth.

25. The enlightenment of a *shravaka,* the enlightenment of a *pratyekabuddha,* and the enlightenment of a *bodhisattva.*

26. That is, the mental state of the gods of the fourth level of the realm of form according to the Abhidharma cosmology.

27. Only when embraced by the sixth paramita of knowledge can the other five trainings such as generosity and so forth be called actual paramitas.

28. In the Tibetan text, Atisha's words are followed by a statement by Potowa that I have unfortunately been unable to resolve. The Tibetan reads as follows: pu to bas kyang/ /rnyed sogs bzhi po gzhan la snang yang/ /de nyid shi zin 'dra bar shes bya/ /mdo smad jo bos sprang mar blangs bzhin/ /de bas rnyed sogs bzhi la dgrar gzung/ A possible interpretation (for which I am indebted to Geshe Tsulga of Sera Je Trehor Khamtsen) is as follows: "Whenever any of the worldly concerns, such as longing for gain, etc., arise in your mind, do not fall under their control but instead remain

like a corpse. If you fall under the sway of the worldly concerns, you will not gain the happiness you desire, and you will find only undesired suffering. It is like the story of the man named Jowo from Amdo who craved honey and went to fetch it from the honeycomb. Instead of getting his longed-for honey, he was stung by the honey bees and suffered terribly. Therefore, always see the eight worldly concerns as enemies."

29. While the miraculous tree bears fruit continuously, the plantain tree grows fruit once and then never again.

# GLOSSARY

**Abhidharma** (Tib. *chos mgon pa*). Buddhist psychology and metaphysics. The third section of the Tripitaka.

**arhat** (Tib. *dgra bcom pa*). Literally, "foe destroyer"; an individual who has realized the absence of personal self and has attained nirvana, the fourth and final result that is specific to the Hinayana path.

**Atisha** (Skt. *atiśa;* Tib. *jo bo rje*) (982–1055). A great Indian master who was one of the primary teachers at Vikramaśīla University, Atisha was also known as Dipaṃkara. Having received many teachings on bodhichitta from important masters, he was invited by the king of Western Tibet to revive Buddhism in Tibet. Author of *The Lamp for the Path to Enlightenment (Bodhipathapradīpa)* and other important texts, Atisha's foremost Tibetan student Dromtonpa founded the Kadam lineage. The mind training lineage started with Atisha and continued with Dromtonpa and his student Potowa.

**Avalokiteshvara** (Skt. *avalokiteśvara;* Tib. *spyan ras gzigs*). The bodhisattva embodying enlightened loving-kindness and compassion.

**Ben Kungyal** (Tib. *'ban kung rgyal*) (eleventh century). Also known as Geshe Ben; a student of Gonpawa.

**Bhrikuti** (Skt. *bhṛkuṭī;* Tib. *khro gnyer can*). A wrathful manifestation of Tara.

**bhumi** (Skt. bhūmi; Tib. sa). Lit. grounds. Stages in the unfolding of bodhisattvas' qualities. Beginning with their first direct perception of the innate nature, bodhisattvas traverse ten bhumis until they reach complete enlightenment.

**bliss-gone one** (Skt. *sugata;* Tib. *bde bar bshegs pa*). An epithet for a buddha.

**Bodhgaya** (Tib. *rdo rje gdan*). The place where Buddha Shakyamuni gained enlightenment. Bodhgaya is situated in northern India in the modern state of Bihar.

**bodhichitta** (Skt. *bodhicitta;* Tib. *byang chub kyi sems*). The mind of enlightenment, the aspiration to attain enlightenment for the sake of all beings.

**bodhisattva** (Tib. *byang chub sems dpa'*). A person who has developed bodhichitta. A practitioner of the Mahayana path, especially one who has attained the first *bhumi.*

**buddha** (Tib. *sangs rgyas*). An enlightened or awakened being who has completely abandoned all obscurations and perfected every good quality. A perfect bodhisattva, after attaining complete and true enlightenment, becomes a buddha. Shakyamuni Buddha, the buddha of this era, lived in India approximately in the sixth century B.C.E. There have been innumerable buddhas in past eons who have manifested the way to enlightenment. In the current eon, there will be one thousand buddhas, of which Buddha Shakyamuni is the fourth.

**Chagtri Chog** (Tib. *phyag khri mchog*) (eleventh century). A great yogi who was a disciple of Lord Atisha.

**Chekawa Yeshe Dorje** (Tib. *mchad kha ba ye shes rdo rje*) (1101–75). Kadam master who systematized the teachings on mind training in the text called the *Seven Points of Mind Training (blo sbyong don bdun ma).* Chekawa was a student of Sharawa.

**Chen-ngawa** (Tib. *spyan snga ba*) (1033–1103). Famous Kadam master. One of the foremost disciples of Dromtonpa and one of the three brothers. Chen-ngawa started the transmission lineage of the oral instructions of the Kadam teachings.

**cyclic existence.** *See* **samsara**.

**dakini** (Skt. *dākinī;* Tib. *mkha' gro ma*). A female principle signifying emptiness and wisdom.

**Dharma** (Tib. *chos*). Generally refers to the Buddha's teachings; may also mean phenomena, attributes, qualities, or mental objects.

**dharmakaya** (Skt. *dharmakāya;* Tib. *chos sku*). The body of qualities which is the mental or nonmanifest aspect of the enlightened mind. It signifies the mind of a buddha, enlightenment itself, unoriginated, primordial mind, devoid of mental constructs, denoting the ultimate nature.

**Dharma Lord Gotsang** (Tib. *chos rjes rgod tshang*) (1189–1258). Kadam master.

**Dolpa** (Tib. *dol pa*) (1059–1131). Geshe Dolpa, a Kadam master who composed the *Blue Udder* and was a disciple of Potowa.

**Dragyabpa** (Tib. *brag rgyab pa*) (eleventh century). Student of Atisha.

**Drogon.** Many masters carry this title, and it is not clear whom Chökyi Dragpa is referring to here.

**Dromtonpa** (Tib. *'brom ston pa*) (1005–64). Founder of the Kadam lineage and foremost Tibetan student of Atisha who was instrumental in persuading Atisha to stay on in Tibet.

**dualistic fixation** (Tib. *gnyis 'dzin*). Mental dichotomy of subject and object; experience structured as "perceiver and perceived."

**ego-clinging** (Tib. *bdag 'dzin*). The habitual clinging to the mistaken idea that the "I" is an independent, singular, and ongoing entity. Ego-clinging is the source of the disturbing emotions and the basis for all the negative karmic actions leading to endless cyclic existence.

**emptiness** (Skt. *śūnyatā;* Tib. *stong pa nyid*). The state of all phenomena as being empty of, or lacking, independent true existence.

**enlightenment** (Skt. *bodhi;* Tib. *byang chub*). Usually the same as the state of buddhahood, characterized by the perfection of the accumulations of merit and wisdom and by the removal of the two obscurations. Sometimes used to imply as well the lower stages of liberation of an *arhat* or a *pratyekabuddha.*

**eternalism** (Skt. *śāśvatānta;* Tib. *rtag lta*). Believing something to be enduring or permanent.

**extreme of existence** (Tib. *srid pa'i mtha'*). Samsara, the opposite of the extreme of nirvanic peace; enlightenment is not confined to either of these two extremes.

**extreme of nihilism** (Skt. *ucchedānta;* Tib. *chad mtha'*). The belief that there are no past and future lives and the disregard of karma—cause and effect. On a more subtle level, the belief that something comes to an end.

**extreme of peace** (Tib. *zhi ba'i mtha'*). The opposite of the extreme of existence; enlightenment transcends both extremes.

**five aggregates** (Skt. *pañaskandha;* Tib. *phung po lnga*). The aggregates of form, feeling, perception, mental formations, and consciousness. Based on these, sentient beings impute personal identity.

**five kinds of diligence.** (1) armor-like diligence, (2) diligence of application, (3) undeterred diligence, (4) irreversible diligence, (5) insatiable diligence.

**formless realm** (Skt. *arūpadhātu;* Tib. *gzugs med khams*). The most subtle state of cyclic existence, without any physical element at all. Lacking even mental pleasure, its beings dwell in unchanging equanimity.

**four activities** (Tib. *spyod lam rnam bzhi*). Daily activities, which are usually enumerated as walking, moving around, lying, and sitting.

**four causes** (Tib. *rgyu bzhi*). (1) Knowing sentient beings to be one's mothers, (2) remembering their kindness, (3) repaying their kindness, and (4) developing superior intentions.

**four extremes** (Tib. *mtha' bzhi*). The ontological extremes involved in the assertions of existence, nonexistence, both existence and nonexistence, and neither existence nor nonexistence.

**four liberations of Shakya Shri.** No information available.

**four meaningful means of magnetizing.** The actual term is "four means of magnetizing," but in the passage Chökyi Dragpa adds *don che ba* ("meaningful" or "which have a great purpose") to the usual term. In Chökyi Nyima Rinpoche's introduction they are explained as (1) being generous, (2) speaking kind words, (3) giving appropriate teachings, and (4) maintaining consistency between one's words and actions.

**four noble truths** (Skt. *catuḥsatya;* Tib. *bden pa bzhi*). The truth of suffering, the truth of the origin of suffering, the truth of cessation, and the truth of the path.

**geshe** (Skt. *kalyānamitra;* Tib. *dge bshes [dge ba'i bshes gnyen]*). Literally, "spiritual friend." Common appellation for a Kadam teacher. Nowadays the title is given to a monk who has earned the degree of Geshe through the Gelug educational system.

**Geshe Nambarwa.** No information available on this figure.

**Geshe Namo.** No information available on this figure.

**giving and receiving** (Tib. *gtong len*). The practice of taking in all the misery and nonvirtue of all sentient beings while breathing in and sending out all one's own happiness and virtues while breathing out.

**Gonpawa** (Tib. *dgon pa ba*) (1016–82). Also known as Dzeng Wangchug Gyaltsen (*'dzeng dbang phyug rgyal mtshan*). One of Atisha's disciples who carried on the lineage of the Kadam *lamrim,* or stages of the path.

**Great Hearing Lineage** (Tib. *snyan brgyud chen mo*). A lineage of instructions passing orally from teacher to disciple.

**Great Perfection** (Tib. *rdzogs pa chen po*). According to the Nyingma school, the pinnacle of all vehicles.

**Great Vehicle**. *See* **Mahayana**.

**Gyalse Togme** (Tib. *rgyal sras mtogs med*) (1295–1369). Kadam master and the author of the root text, *The Thirty-Seven Practices of a Bodhisattva (rgyal ba'i sras kyi lag len sum chu so bdun ma); also known as Togme Zangpo.

**higher realms** (Skt. *svarga;* Tib. *mtho ris*). The three higher realms of humans, demigods, and gods.

**Hinayana** (Skt. *hīnayāna;* Tib. *theg pa dman pa*). Literally, "small vehicle." Vehicle of the *shravaka* and *pratyekabuddhas,* for whom the main pursuit is the achievement of individual liberation.

**hungry ghost** (Skt. *preta;* Tib. *yi dvags*). One of the six classes of sentient beings. These beings are tormented by their impure karmic perception, causing them to suffer tremendously from craving, hunger, and thirst.

**Indra** (Tib. *lha'i dbang po*). Literally, "king of the gods," he resides in the realm of desire in palace on the summit of the central mountain, Mount Meru.

**Ishvara** (Skt. *īśvara;* Tib. *dbangs phyug*). The Almighty, a Hindu creator god.

**Jayulwa** (Tib. *bya yul ba*) (1075–1138). Famous Kadam master.

**Kadam lineage** (Tib. *bka' gdams*). Founded by Dromtonpa, student of Atisha. Usually depicted as a reformist school that undertook as one of its more important missions the presentation of the fundamentals of Buddhism in a manner easily accessible to the clergy and educated laity. Following the teachings of Atisha, it stressed compassion, study, and pure discipline. The Kadam teachings were absorbed into all other schools of Buddhism in Tibet as those schools emulated the monastic model provided by the Kadam school.

**Kamapa** (Tib. *ka ma pa shes rab 'od*) (1057–1131). Kamapa was a disciple Gonpawa.

**karma** (Tib. *las*). Literally "action." Physical, verbal, or mental acts that imprint habitual tendencies in the mind.

**karshapana** (Skt. *kārṣāpaṇa*). Currency used in ancient India.

**kaya** (Skt. *kāya;* Tib. *sku*). Literally "body," but in the sense of a body or embodiment of numerous qualities. The two kayas are *rupakaya,* or form body, and *dharmakaya,* or body of qualities.

**Khamlungpa** (Tib. *khams lung pa*) (1085–1175). Kadam master famed for his compassion and loving-kindness.

**Kharagpa Gomchung** (Tib. *kha rag pa sgom chung*) (eleventh century). Literally, "little meditator of Kharag." A Kadam master and disciple of Potowa. Kharagpa is famous for his perseverance and strict application of the teachings. It is said that he received teachings on the Great Perfection and attained the rainbow body.

**Kyangtsa Doltsul** (Tib. *rkyang tsha rdol tshul*) (eleventh–twelfth century). Disciple of Potowa.

**lama** (Skt. *guru;* Tib. *bla ma*). A spiritual teacher.

**Langri Tangpa** (Tib. *glang ri thang pa*) (1054–1123). Author of the first text, *The Eight Stanzas of Mind Training (blo sbyong tshigs brgyad ma),* to actually bear the name "mind training" *(blo sbyong)*. Teacher of Sharawa and a disciple of Geshe Potowa. Founder of Langtang Monastery.

**liberation** (Skt. *mokṣa;* Tib. *thar pa*). Emancipation from cyclic existence.

**Lord of Secrets** (Skt. *guhyapati;* Tib. *gsang ba'i bdag po*). Epithet for Vajrapani.

**lower realms** (Skt. *apāya;* Tib. *ngan song*). The three suffering abodes of hell beings, hungry ghosts, and animals.

**Mahayana** (Skt. *mahāyāna;* Tib. *theg pa chen po*). The "Great Vehicle" of bodhisattvas, who strive for perfect enlightenment for the benefit of all sentient beings.

**Maitreya** (Tib. *byams pa*). Buddha of the future, the fifth in this present eon; Maitreya is presently Buddha Shakyamuni's regent.

**mandala** (Skt. *maṇḍala;* Tib. *dkyil 'khor*). Literally, "center and periphery"; in the ceremonial context it refers to a symbolic offering of the entire universe.

**Manjushri** (Skt. *mañjuśrī;* Tib. *'jam dpal dbyangs*). The bodhisattva embodying wisdom and supreme knowledge.

**meditative equipoise** (Tib. *mnyam gzhag*). Resting in the composure of meditation. May also refer to the occasion of realizing the nature of things directly.

**Middle Way** (Skt. *madhyamaka;* Tib. *dbu ma*). Philosophical perspective of the Great Vehicle. Through logical arguments the conceptual mind is deconstructed, thereby allowing for the realization of the emptiness of all phenomena.

**mind of enlightenment.** *See* **bodhichitta.**

**Mount Meru** (Tib. *ri rab*). The central king of mountains in Buddhist Abhidharma cosmology.

**naga** (Skt. *nāga;* Tib. *klu*). Beings with snakelike bodies who may be either benevolent or malicious and are often associated with guarding the earth's treasures.

**Nagarjuna** (Skt. *nāgārjuna;* Tib. *klu grub*). Famous Indian master, who lived possibly in the second century. Founder of the Middle Way school and author of numerous scriptures on philosophical and medical topics.

**Naljorpa Chenpo** (Tib. *rnal 'byor pa chen po*) (1016–1078). A Kadam master and student of Atisha who assumed Dromtonpa's seat after Dromtonpa passed away in 1065.

**Neuzurpa** (Tib. *sne'u zur pa*) (1042–1118). Kadam master and a disciple of Gonpawa.

**Ngulchu Togme** (Tib. *dngul chu mtogs med*). *See* **Gyalse Togme.**

**nirvana** (Skt. *nirvāṇa;* Tib. *myang 'das*). The extinguishing of the causes for cyclic existence. The lesser nirvana refers to the liberation from cyclic existence attained by a Hinayana practitioner. When referring to a buddha, nirvana is the great nondwelling state of enlightenment that falls neither in the extreme of samsaric existence nor in the passive state of cessation attained by an *arhat.*

**Nyetang** (Tib. *snye thang*). Place in Central Tibet *(dbus)*. Atisha passed away in Nyetang.

**Nyugrumpa** (Tib. *nyug rum pa*). Kadam master who passed away in the year 1175.

**paramita** (Skt. *pāramitā;* Tib. *pha rol tu phyin pa drug*). Literally, "reaching the other shore"; refers primarily to the six transcendent actions of generosity, discipline, patience, diligence, meditative concentration, and knowledge.

**Pitaka.** *See* **Tripitaka.**

**post-meditation** (Tib. *rjes thob*). Literally, "ensuing attainment"; the state between periods of meditative equipoise.

**Potowa** (Tib. *po to ba rin chen gsal*) (1027–1105). Chief disciple of Dromtonpa and one of the three brothers; author of *Dharma through Example (Dpe chos)*.

**pratyekabuddha** (Tib. *rang sangs rgyas*). Literally, "solitarily enlightened one." One who has reached perfection in the second Hinayana vehicle, chiefly through contemplation of the twelve links of dependent origination in reverse order.

**Puchungwa** (Tib. *phu chung ba*) (1031–1106). Kadam master; one of the chief disciples of Dromtonpa and one of the three brothers.

**pure conduct** (Skt. *brahmacaryā;* Tib. *tshang spyod*). Literally, "the conduct of Brahma," implying celibacy.

**Radreng** (Tib. *rva sgreng*). Monastery founded by Dromtonpa in 1057, that was the main seat of the Kadam order until the fifteenth century. Often pronounced and spelled "Reting."

**rainbow body** (Tib. *'ja' lus*). When a practitioner who has gained deep realization through the practice of the Great Perfection passes away, the five elements that form the physical body dissolve back into their essences, i.e., five-colored rainbow light.

**Rinchen Gangpa** (Tib. *rin chen sgang pa*) (1245–1302). Kadampa master.

**rinpoche** (Tib. *rin po che*). Literally, "precious one." An honorific term for a Tibetan lama.

**rupakaya** (Skt. *rūpakāya;* Tib. *gzugs sku*). The form body, rupakaya, is a collective term for the unity of the *sambhogakaya* and *nirmanakaya*.

**Sage** (Skt. *muni;* Tib. *thub pa*). Epithet for the Buddha.

**samadhi** (Skt. *samādhi;* Tib. *ting nge 'dzin*). Meditating evenly. Here often translated as meditative absorption.

**Samantabhadra** (Tib. *kun tu bzang po*). One of the eight great bodhisattvas and an emanation of Vajrasattva.

**samaya** (Tib. *dam tshig*). Commitments of a Vajrayana practitioner. The Vajrayana enumerates numerous such commitments, yet they may all be said to be observed when the practitioner does not part from the perception of appearance being the vajra body of visible emptiness, sound being the vajra speech of audible emptiness, and mind and mental events being the vajra mind of aware emptiness.

**sambhogakaya** (Skt. *sambhogakāya;* Tib. *long spyod rdzogs pa'i sku*). Body of complete enjoyment. Empty yet apparent body of a Buddha manifesting to teach noble beings. Also refers to the luminous aspect of enlightenment.

**samsara** (Skt. *saṃsāra;* Tib. *'khor ba*). Cyclic existence, vicious circle, or round of birth and death and rebirth within the six realms of existence, characterized by suffering, impermanence, and ignorance. The state of ordinary sentient beings fettered by ignorance and dualistic perception, karma, and disturbing emotions.

**Sangha** (Skt. *saṅgha;* Tib. *dge 'dun*). Followers of the Buddha who can guide others on the path. It refers to *arhats* and bodhisattvas, or to a gathering of four or more ordained monks and nuns. It is sometimes used more broadly to refer to all practitioners of the Buddhist teachings.

**selflessness** (Skt. *anātmaka;* Tib. *bdag med*). The absence or lack of a self-entity of the individual person as well as of matter and mind. Selflessness is the natural state of all phenomena.

**seven instructions.** No information available.

**Shabopa** (Tib. *sha bo pa*) (1067–1131). Shabo Gangpa Pema Tsultrim (*sha bo sgang pa pad ma tshul khrims*); Kadam master.

**Sharawa** (Tib. *sha ra ba*) (1070–1141). Kadam master who was a student of Langri Tangpa and Potowa and the teacher of Chekawa.

**Shenton.** No information available on this figure.

**shravaka** (Skt. *śravaka;* Tib. *nyan thos*). Literally, "hearer." One who listens to the teachings of the Buddha, realizes the suffering inherent in samsara, and focuses on understanding that there is no independent self. By conquering emotions, he liberates himself, attaining first the stage of stream enterer at the path of seeing, followed by the stage of once-returner who will be reborn only one more time in the desire realm, and finally the stage of nonreturner who will no longer be reborn into samsara. The final goal is to become an *arhat.* The vehicle of the shravaka is known as the *shravakayana.*

**Shri Sambhava** (Tib. *dpal 'byung ba*). *The Biography of Shri Sambhava* (Skt. Śrīsambhavavimokṣa) is a chapter in the *Sutra of the Ornamental Display (Gaṇḍavyūhasūtra).*

**sutra** (Skt. *sūtra;* Tib. *mdo*). Discourse or teaching by the Buddha belonging to the Tripitaka; also refers to all causal teachings that regard the path as the cause for enlightenment.

**tantra** (Tib. *rgyud*). Literally, "continuity"; the Vajrayana teachings given by the Buddha in his sambhogakaya form. Generally refers to the extraordinary tantric scriptures that are exalted above the sutras.

**Tara** (Skt. *tārā;* Tib. *sgrol ma*). Female bodhisattva born from a tear of Avalokiteshvara. Female manifestation of great compassion and enlightenment.

**tathagata** (Skt. *tathāgata;* Tib. *de bzhin gshegs pa*). Literally, "thus-gone one"; epithet of the Buddha.

**Tazhi** (Tib. *mtha' bzhi*). Tazhi is his title, while his real name is Tong Sumgangwa (*stong gsum gang ba*); no dates available.

**ten directions** (Tib. *phyogs bcu*). The four cardinal directions, the four intermediate ones, upward, and downward.

**ten nonvirtues** (Tib. *mi dge ba bcu*). The nonvirtuous actions of body are killing, taking what has not been given, and engaging in sexual misconduct. The nonvirtuous actions of speech are lying, uttering divisive talk, harsh words, and gossip. The nonvirtuous actions of mind are covetousness, ill will, and wrong views.

**ten virtuous deeds** (Tib. *dge ba bcu*). Generally, to refrain from the above ten nonvirtuous actions and engage in their opposites.

**three brothers** (Tib. *kum ched gsum*). The three foremost disciples of Dromtonpa, namely Puchungwa, Potowa, and Chen-ngawa.

**three doors** (Tib. *sgo gsum*). The three ways to accumulate karmic seeds, i.e., though actions of body, speech, and mind.

**Three Jewels** (Skt. *triratna;* Tib. *dkon mchog gsum*). The Buddha, Dharma, and Sangha.

**three poisons** (Tib. *dug gsum*) The mental poisons of attachment, anger, and stupidity.

**three realms of existence** (Skt. *tribhava;* Tib. *srid pa gsum*). Synonym for the three realms *(khams gsum),* the desire, form, and formless realms.

**three spheres** (Skt. *trimaṇḍala;* Tib. *'khor gsum*). The conceptualizations pertaining to subject, object, and action.

**three times** (Tib. *dus gsum*) Past, present, and future.

**three trainings** (Tib. *bslab pa gsum*). Discipline, meditation, and knowledge.

**Togme; Togme Zangpo.** *See* **Gyalse Togme**.

**torma** (Skt. *bali;* Tib. *gtor ma*). Ritual symbols, often constructed of dough and butter, used as offerings or to represent deities.

**Tripitaka** (Skt. *tripiṭaka;* Tib. *sde snod*). Literally, "three receptacles"; refers to the three collections of Buddha's teachings, the Vinaya, Abhidharma, and Sutra.

**truth of origin** (Skt. *samudayasatya;* Tib. *kun 'byung bden pa*). The second among the four noble truths: the origin of suffering is karma and disturbing emotions.

**truth of suffering** (Skt. *duḥkhasatya;* Tib. *sdug bden*). The first among the four noble truths: everything defiling is painful.

**twelve practices of the Dharma Lord Gotsang.** No information available.

**two accumulations** (Skt. *divarga;* Tib. *tsogs gnyis*). The accumulation of merit with concepts and of wisdom beyond concepts.

**two benefits** (Tib. *don gnyis*). The benefit for oneself and the benefit for others.

**two kayas**. *See* **kaya.**

**two obscurations** (Tib. *sgrib pa gnyis*). The obscurations of the coarse negative emotions and the cognitive obscurations consisting of dualistic concepts.

**Vaishravana** (Skt. *vaiśravaṇa;* Tib. *rnam thos bu*). Guardian of the north and a wealth god.

**Vajra** (Tib. *rdo rje*). Symbol for indestructible wisdom. A symbolic vajra is used as an instrument in tantric rituals in combination with a bell (as depicted on the cover of this book). Bell and vajra together symbolize the unity of wisdom and compassion.

**Vajrapani** (Skt. *vajrapāṇi;* Tib. *phyag na rdo rje*). The bodhisattva embodying enlightened power. In his right hand he carries a flaming pointed *vajra,* and in his left he holds the king of eagles.

**Vajrasattva** (Tib. *rdo rje sems pa'*). A buddha of the vajra family. Vajrasattva is white and is associated with purity and purification.

**Vajrayana** (Skt. *vajrayāna;* Tib. *rdo rje theg pa*). Vehicle that takes the result as the path. Its teachings are the corpus of tantras.

**Vinaya** (Tib. *'dul ba*). The Buddha's teachings of discipline and moral conduct that are the foundation for all Dharma practice, both for lay and ordained people. One of the three parts of the Tripitaka.

**Yerba Shangtsun** (Tib. *yer ba'i zhang btsun*) (eleventh century). Disciple of Atisha.

**yidam deity** (Skt. *adhideva;* Tib. *lhag pa'i lha*). A practitioner's personal deity and, among the three roots, the root of accomplishment.

**yoga** (Tib. *rnal 'byor*). Literally, "uniting (*'byor*) in naturalness (*rnal*)."

# SOURCES CITED

D = *From the Derge Edition of the Tibetan Tripiṭaka*

*Abhidharma Compendium*, D4049 (Skt. *Abhidharmasamuccaya*; Tib. *Mngon pa kun btus*) by Asaṅga.

*Abhidharma Treasury*, D4089 (Skt. *Abhidharmakośa*; Tib. *Mngon pa mdzod*) by Vasubandhu.

*Blue Udder* (Tib. *Be'u bum sngon po*) by Geshe Dolpa (dge bshes dol pa).

*Bodhisattva Pitaka*, D56 (Skt. *Bodhisattvapiṭaka*; Tib. *Byang chub sems dpa'i sde snod*).

*Commentary on the Enlightened Mind*, D1800 (Skt. *Bodhicittavivaraṇa*; Tib. *Byang chub sems kyi 'grel pa*) by Nāgārjuna.

*Compendium of Trainings*, D3940 (Skt. *Śikṣāsamuccaya*; Tib. *Slab btus*) by Śāntideva.

*Dharma through Example* (Tib. *Dpe chos*) by Potowa (po to ba).

*Enlightenment of Vairochana, The*, D494 (Skt. *Mahāvairocānabhisambodhi*; Tib. *Rnam snang mgon byang*).

*Entering into the Middle Way*, D3861 (Skt. *Madhyamakāvatāra;* Tib. *Dbu ma la 'jug pa*) by Candrakīrti.

*Essence of the Middle Way*, D3855 (Skt. *Madhyamakahṛdayakārikā*; Tib. *Dbu ma snyin po*) by Bhāvaviveka.

*Four Hundred Verses of the Middle Way*, D3846 (Skt. *Catuḥśataka*; Tib. *Dbu ma bzhi brgya pa*) by Āryadeva.

*Hundred Verses*, D4332 (Skt. *Śatagāthā*; Tib. *Tshig bcad brgya pa*) by Vararuci.

*Individual Liberation of the Bodhisattva*. No information available.

*Jataka Stories*, D32 (Skt. *Jātakanidāna*; Tib. *Skyes rabs*).

*King of Samadhi Sutra*, D127 (Skt. *Samādhirājasūtra*; Tib. *Ting 'dzin rgyal po*).

*Letter to a Friend*, D4182 (Skt. *Suhṛllekha*; Tib. *Bshes springs*) by Nāgārjuna.

*Method for Accomplishing the Path of the Mahayana*, D3954 (Skt. *Mahāyānapathasādhana*; Tib. *Teg chen lam gyi sgrub thabs*) by Atiśa.

203

*Mind Training* (Tib. *Blo sbyong*) refers here to *The Wheel-Weapon Mind Training (Blo sbyong mtshon cha 'i khor lo)*, attributed to the Indian teacher Dharmarakṣita.

*Moon Lamp Sutra* (Tib. *Zla ba sgron me mdo*). See *King of Samadhi Sutra.*

*Nirvana Sutra*, D120 (Skt. *Mahāparinirvāṇasūtra*; Tib. *Mya ngan las 'das pa'i mdo*).

*Ornament of the Sutras*, D4020 (Skt. *Sūtrālaṃkāra*; Tib. *Mdo sde'i rgyan*) by Maitreya.

*Paramita Compendium, The,* D3944 (Skt. *Pāramitāsamāsa*; Tib. *Phar phyin bsdus pa*) by Āryaśūra.

*Precious Garland of the Middle Way*, D4158 (Skt. *Rājaparikathāratnamālā*; Tib. *Dbu ma rin chen phreng ba*) by Nāgārjuna.

*Purposeful Expressions*, D4099 (Skt. *Udānavarga;* Tib. *Ched du mjod pa'i mtshoms)* compiled by Dharmattrāta.

*Questions and Answers of the Father Teaching, The,* (Tib. *Pha chos zhu len*) by Dromtonpa ('Brom ston pa).

*Seal Sutra of the Development of Faithful Strength,* D201 (Skt. *Śraddhābalādhānāvatarāmudrāsūtra*; Tib. *Dad pa'i stobs bskyed pa la 'jug pa'i phyag rgya zhes bya ba'i mdo*).

*Seal Sutra That Regards Certainty and Uncertainty,* D202 (Skt. *Niyatāniyaragatimudrāvatarāsūtra*; Tib. *Nges pa dang ma nges par 'gro ba'i phyag rgya la 'jug pa zhes bya ba'i mdo*).

*Seventy Admonitions* (Tib. *Am yig dun chu pa*) by Kharagpa (kha rag pa).

*Seventy Stanzas of Taking Refuge*, D3971 (Skt. *Triśaraṇagamanasaptati*; Tib. *Skyabs 'gro bdun cu pa*) by Candrakīrti.

*Supreme Continuity, The,* D4024 (Skt. *Uttaratantraśāstra*; Tib. *Rgyud bla ma*) by Maitreya.

*Supreme Jeweled Cloud Sutra*, D231 (Skt. *Ratnameghasūtra*; Tib. *Dkon mchog sprin*).

*Sutra of the Application of Mindfulness*, D287 (Skt. *Smṛtyupasthānasūtra;* Tib. *Dran pa nyer bzhag mdo*).

*Sutra of the Authentic Compilation of All Phenomena*, D238 (Skt. *Dharmasaṃgītisūtra;* Tib. *Chos thams cad yang dag par sdud pa'i mdo*).

*Sutra of Completely Pure Conduct.* No information available.

*Sutra of the Great Display*, D95 (Skt. *Lalitavistarasūtra;* Tib. *Rgya cher rol pa*).

*Sutra Inspiring Supreme Intention*, D69 (Skt. *Adhyāśāyasaṃcodanasūtra*; Tib. *Lhag bsam bskul ba'i mdo*).

*Sutra of Instructions to the King*, D214 (Skt. *Rājādeśasūtra;* Tib. *Rgyal po la gdams pa'i mdo*).

*Sutra of the Magical Ascertainment of Utter Peace*, D129 (Skt. *Praśāntaviniścayaprātihāryasamādhisūtra;* Tib. *Rab tu zhi ba rnam par nges pa'i chos 'phrul gyi mdo*).

*Sutra of the Ornamental Array*, D44, 45 (Skt. *Gaṇḍavyūhasūtra;* Tib. *Sdong po bkod pa'i mdo*).

*Sutra Requested by the Householder Ugra*, D63 *(Skt. Gṛhapati ugrapariprcchāsūtra; Tib. Drag shul chen gyis zhus pa'i mdo).*

*Sutra Requested by Inexhaustible Intelligence*, D152 (Skt. *Sāgaramatiparipṛcchāsūtra;* Tib. *Blo gros rgya mtshos zhus pa'i mdo*).

*Sutra Requested by Kashyapa*, D40 (Skt. *Mahākāśyapasūtra;* Tib. *'Od srung kyis zhus pa'i mdo*).

*Sutra Requested by Narayana*, D684 (Skt. *Nārāyaṇaparipṛcchāsūtra;* Tib. *Sred med kyi bus zhus pa'i mdo*).

Sutra Requested by Shridatta, D72 (Skt. VīradattagṛhapatiparipṛcchᵥsOtra; Tib. Dpal byin gyis zhus pa'i mdo).

*Treasure of Precious Well-Spoken Statements, The, (Tib. Legs bshad rin po che'i gter*) by Sakya Pandita (Sas skya paṇḍita).

*Way of the Bodhisattva, The,* D3871 (Skt. *Bodhicaryāvatāra;* Tib. *Spyod 'jug*) by Śāntideva.

# INDEX OF NAMES

# ABOUT THE AUTHORS

TUBTEN CHÖKYI DRAGPA (died c. 1908), also known as Minyag Kunzang Sönam, was the main student from the Gelug school of the illustrious Patrul Rinpoche.

CHÖKYI NYIMA RINPOCHE (1950–) is a renowned contemporary Buddhist teacher who founded and guides the Ranjung Yeshe Institute in Kathmandu, Nepal. He is the author of *The Union of Mahamudra and Dzogchen*.

HEIDI I. KÖPPL has translated for Tibetan lamas in Kathmandu for many years and has a degree in Tibetology from the University of Copenhagen.

### Creation and Completion:
### Essential Points of Tantric Meditation
Jamgön Kongtrul
Translated and introduced by Sarah Harding
Commentary by Khenchen Thrangu Rinpoche
176 pages, ISBN 0-86171-312-5, $16.95

A classic practice text becomes even more useful:
the inclusion of Rinpoche's commentary makes
the terminology experientially alive. These are
powerful meditation instructions, of immense
value to aspiring and experienced practitioners
alike. Includes Tibetan root text.

### Essentials of Mahamudra:
### Looking Directly at the Mind
Khenchen Thrangu Rinpoche
288 pages, ISBN 0-86171-371-0, $16.95

The Tibetan Buddhist practice of mahamudra can
lead to profound realization, but it is also an infi-
nitely adaptable practice, relevant for today's busy
world. Created by a Tibetan teacher known for
his skill in making teachings clear for Western
students, *Essentials of Mahamudra* is unmatched in
its directness.

### World of Tibetan Buddhism
His Holiness the Dalai Lama
224 pages, ISBN 0-86171-097-5, $15.95

"The definitive book on Tibetan Buddhism by
the world's ultimate authority."
—The Reader's Review

"A rare and marvelous opportunity for English-
language readers to learn more about [Tibetan
Buddhism and its] spiritual leader."
—*Library Journal*

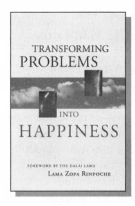

## Transforming Problems into Happiness

Lama Thubten Zopa Rinpoche
104 pages, ISBN 0-86171-194-7, $12.95

"A masterfully brief statement of Buddhist teachings on the nature of humanity and human suffering. The ancient technique is given a fresh and practical treatment here. *Transforming Problems* offers scripts you can use almost like mantras to direct the mind: 'Think how this problem will help you eliminate pride.' 'Think how you could change your behavior.' This book should be read as the words of a wise, loving parent whose sternness underlines the importance of what is being taught."—*Utne Reader*

## Natural Liberation: Padmasambhava's Teachings on the Six Bardos

Padmasambhava
Commentary by Gyatrul Rinoche
Translated by B. Alan Wallace
272 pages, ISBN 0-86171-131-9, $16.95

Padmasambhava, the great ninth-century Indian master who established Buddhism in Tibet, describes in detail six life-processes, or *bardos,* and how to transform them into vehicles for enlightenment. This most extraordinary teaching is here accompanied by meditation instructions and edifying anecdotes in a lucid commentary by Gyatrul Rinpoche, an esteemed teacher of the Nyingma tradition.

## Introduction to Tantra:
## The Transformation of Desire
Edited by Jonathan Landaw
Foreword by Philip Glass
192 pages, ISBN 0-86171-162-9, $16.95

Tantra—so often misunderstood—is presented as
a practice leading to joy and self-discovery, with a
vision of reality that is simple, clear, and relevant
to our lives.

"The best introductory work on Tibetan Buddhist
tantra available, readily accessible to Western
students."—Professor Janet Gyatso, Hershey
Chair of Buddhist Studies, Harvard University

## Luminous Mind:
## The Way of the Buddha
Kalu Rinpoche
Foreword by His Holiness the Dalai Lama
352 pages, ISBN 0-86171-118-1, $19.95

A remarkable compilation of the oral and written
teachings of the late Kalu Rinpoche—who was
called "a beacon of inspiration" by the Dalai
Lama. Kalu Rinpoche taught with an inviting,
playful, and lucid style that was just one natural
manifestation of his own profound realization.
The teachings presented in *Luminous Mind* are
immediate and timeless.

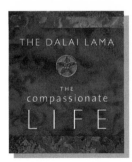

## The Compassionate Life
The Dalai Lama
128 pages, ISBN 0-86171-378-8, $11.95

"It is all here, everything we need to enact in our
own lives, even in the most trying of times, if we
are to realize the possibilities of true happiness in
this very life. A sorely-needed prescription for sani-
ty and kindness in the world."—Jon Kabat-Zinn,
author of *Wherever You Go, There You Are*

## Peacock in the Poison Grove:
## Two Buddhist Texts for Training the Mind
Geshe Lhundub Sopa
with Michael Sweet and Leonard Zwilling
320 pages, ISBN 0-86171-185-8, $19.95

"The two long poems translated here, attributed to Atisha's guru, Dharmarakshita, are among the oldest and most dramatic of the mind-training texts, woven as they are of startling imagery and a quintessentially Tibetan admixture of sutra and tantra practices, as well as conventional and ultimate perspectives on the world. *Peacock in the Poison Grove* provides lucid translations of the texts, and a humane and learned commentary revealing why Geshe Sopa has long been regarded as one of the greatest living scholars of Tibetan Buddhism. This book belongs on the shelf—and a readily accessible one at that!—of every scholar and practitioner of Tibetan Buddhism."
—Professor Roger Jackson, Carleton College, author of *Is Enlightenment Possible?*

## Advice from a Spiritual Friend
Geshe Rabten and Geshe Dhargyey
Introduction by Stephen Batchelor
176 pages, ISBN 0-86171-193-9, $15.95

Based on practical Buddhist verses on "thought training," *Advice from a Spiritual Friend* teaches how to develop the inner skills that lead to contentment by responding to everyday difficulties with patience and joy.

"Reading this book is akin to taking a personal retreat with two kindly and wise teachers. The instructions for realizing compassion in everyday life are readable and clear, and offer enhanced spiritual skills to readers of any background an orientation."—*NAPRA ReVIEW*

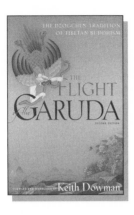

## The Flight of the Garuda:
## The Dzogchen Tradition
## of Tibetan Buddhism
Edited and translated by Keith Dowman
240 pages, ISBN 0-86171-367-2, $16.95

Buddhists of all stripes will find ample sustenance
in these lyrical forays into the Dzogchen view.
This new edition of Dowman's concise and
valuable introduction contains translations of
five essential texts, including on not previously
available.

## Vast as the Heavens,
## Deep as the Sea:
## Verses in Praise of Bodhicitta
Khunu Rinpoche
160 pages, ISBN 0-86171-146-7, $16.95

"Khunu Rinpoche was a bodhisattva and a saint.
When I first heard of his *Praise of Bodhicitta,* I was
filled with joy: what could be more precious than
a teaching on bodhicitta by someone such as
him? To hold in your hands Khunu Rinpoche's
own words on bodhicitta is to be given a priceless opportunity—of touching the heart of a master who made it the guiding light of his entire
life."—Sogyal Rinpoche, author of *The Tibetan
Book of Living and Dying*

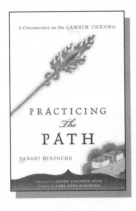

## Practicing the Path:
## A Commentary on the Lamrim Chenmo
Yangsi Rinpoche
Foreword by Geshe Lhundub Sopa
Preface by Lama Zopa Rinpoche
576 pages, ISBN 0-86171-346-X, $24.95

A complete commentary on Lama Tsongkhapa's *Great Exposition on the Stages of the Path* as rendered by a young, contemporary teacher especially known for his eloquence and clarity.

"Readable and to the point, it brings this great classical tradition 'into the very palms of our hands.'"
—Jose Ignacio Cabezon, XIVth Dalai Lama Professor of Tibetan Buddhism and Cultural Studies, University of California, Santa Barbara

## Steps on the Path to Enlightenment
A Commentary on the Lamrim Chenmo, Volume 1
By Geshe Llundub Sopa
Foreword by H.H. the 14th Dalai Lama
556 pages, cloth ISBN 0-86171-346-X, $39.95

Volume I of a comprehensive and authoritative five-volume commentary on The Lamrim Chenmo. This much-anticipated work by the renowned Buddhist scholar, Geshe Sopa, goes into great detail to ensure the greatest understanding of the very long and complex root text.

 # WISDOM PUBLICATIONS